GRACE MOTHERS

LETTERS TO OUR CHILDREN

GRACE MOTHERS

LETTERS TO OUR CHILDREN

FOREWORD

My very favourite family gatherings are christenings. A couple of weeks ago on a gorgeous spring morning we gathered at St John's Cathedral in Brisbane for the baptism of Sylvie Grace Bryce, darling youngest of our 12 grandchildren. Sylvie is one year old, and greatly loved by all around her, most especially her siblings and circle of cousins.

As I sat in the midst of them and the magnificent gothic sandstone arches, beautiful stained-glass windows and glorious music, I felt shrouded in happiness and calm, in mother love.

Children have been my life and my love; not just my own, but all children.

Louis Pasteur put it perfectly: "When I approach a child, he inspires in me two sentiments: tenderness for what he is, and respect for what he may become."

When I became a mother at 23, I embarked on the personal, professional, political engagement that has been my central focus. Of course I did not know all those years ago that it would be so. Again and again I have turned to the Preamble to the United Nations Declaration on the Rights of the Child (1959): '… mankind owes to the child the best it has to give.'

These words have been my source of inspiration, courage and support throughout my career in human rights law and practice, in grassroots community engagement, in public life.

Like grandmothers everywhere in our country and around the world, my priorities are concerned with the future of next generations – our children and our grandchildren.

The wellbeing of mothers is absolutely key. I am deeply impressed by the achievements and contributions of those I observe in 2018 doing their best every day to care for their kids. They do this while juggling an extraordinary range of responsibilities: at home, school, sport, music, study, celebrations, keeping things going… involved in every aspect of our society – giving, loving, sharing. Careers part-time, full-time, some on hold. Countless hours of volunteering, fundraising, hard work and legendary multiskilling.

I have a strong commitment to the continuing struggle for gender equality. Yes, our proud Australian women's movement has notched up many powerful reforms – measures that I never could have imagined when I was a girl – but we have a lot more to do to reach our goals of equality of opportunity and equal status for all women. This includes the support needed to fulfil potential, hopes and aspirations.

It worries me that many mothers carry heavy loads, the way many live on the verge of exhaustion. Often they speak to me of feelings of loneliness and isolation. I am evangelical about the need for them to take good care of themselves. I tell them to throw out those myths of the superwoman, the burnt-chop syndrome, perfectionism, the yummy mummy; to squeeze in some time every day for a few stretches, deep breathing… no matter what. Ten minutes will do.

I urge them to remember that the most important journey is to the centre of oneself. Leave time for the lovely things in life – music, the beauty of nature, art, poetry, friendship, laughter – for the bread and the roses. These are the things that build the store of resilience we need to face the future with confidence and courage.

Follow aviator Amelia Earhart's advice to never say no to a new adventure – be bold, be bold, be bold.

Dame Quentin Bryce AD CVO
25th Governor-General of Australia

INTRODUCTION

When we were on deadline for this book, my nan passed away. She was 93. It was an overwhelmingly sad time; she was like a second mother to me and, even now, I still talk to her every day. It was hard watching her develop dementia. Every time I'd walk into her room, I'd talk to her about the things we'd done together – climbed the Eiffel Tower, explored the streets of Bangkok, shopped in Hong Kong... How she was the first person to feed solids to my firstborn, Arabella. When she passed, I sat next to her bed and thanked her for encouraging me to chase my dreams; to always give things a go.

When I launched *The Grace Tales*, more than five years ago, I was living with my mother, step-dad and nan. We were renovating our family home, so my husband and I, and Arabella, our newborn daughter who refused to sleep, moved in for six months.

Nan used to sit in her sitting room with her Labrador, Max. She'd read the paper, attempt to use the computer that we'd set up for her, or watch one of her favourite programs on the TV (M*A*S*H was always on at night). I remember excitedly telling her about my idea for *The Grace Tales*. She did what she's always done – told me to go for it.

And so I did. I started the business on my laptop. If only she knew I was sitting here, writing the introduction for our first book, she'd be so proud.

Surrounding yourself with women who inspire you will take you far in life. I couldn't have achieved what I have with *The Grace Tales* without the many women who've helped and inspired me (starting with my mother, who is the most inspirational woman I know).

Early on, when I first started planning the launch of *The Grace Tales*, I stumbled across the work of photographer Julie Adams. There was something so beautiful about her imagery and, even now, I can always pick her photographs instantly. Julie's use of light is magical and the way she captures people is extraordinary. We met for coffee.

> *"Each letter is HEARTFELT, emotive, real, HONEST and full of passion and LOVE. My gosh, there's a lot of love."*

I had a reflux-ridden baby on my lap and she'd recently returned home from New York. We connected instantly and so began a very happy working relationship, which turned into a great friendship. Collaborating with Julie on this book has been an absolute joy. (I often tell her she's a "joy spreader" – she has the most wonderful, infectious laugh.)

I first met our UK editor, Claire Brayford, more than a decade ago, when I was living and working in Dubai. She walked into the room in a fabulous camel coat and I remember thinking how chic she looked. We spent the weekend together and, despite living on opposite sides of the world, we've been great friends ever since. Claire's an incredible writer, and working on this book with these women – both dear friends – is a dream come true.

When I started *The Grace Tales*, there was no business plan. At the time, I was working at Australian *Vogue* as the fashion features director and deputy editor, while trying to navigate life with a new baby.

The Grace Tales was escapism for me; it never felt like work. I loved going on photo shoots and treasure the connections I made with the women we profiled. Advice and laughter would fly around the room. We were all in it together. We understood each other without even opening our mouths.

Over the years, I poured so much passion and love into the site that it grew and grew. After my second daughter, Lottie, arrived, I resigned from *Vogue* and closed that chapter of my life. It felt wonderful. No regrets, ever. Another chapter began.

The Grace Tales is the go-to lifestyle destination for style-conscious mothers around the world. Sometimes I can't believe that something I started on my couch has grown into a thriving business. I never saw myself as an entrepreneur, but given that my mother ran her own interior design business for more than 20 years, her determination was bound to rub off on me. She always taught me that you could do anything you put your mind to, and I firmly believe this.

Over the past five years, we have built a wonderful community of like-minded mothers. We've become part of their motherhood journey and we've reminded them that they're not alone. Because there are many moments when you're a mother that you feel alone. Your self-esteem takes a dive, and if women can't talk about what they're experiencing, the isolation can be overwhelming.

From the very beginning, sharing honest stories on the site has been at the heart of what we do. I'm an open book – I tell it like it is – and I wanted the women we featured on the site to do the same. We connect through our vulnerabilities, and being open not only lets you connect to other women, it's also incredibly cathartic.

We've shared the stories of mothers from around the world. We've shared their ups and downs. We've shared their strength and courage. And there's so much bravery in all of us. I wanted to be a mother for longer than I can remember, but I never anticipated how much it would change my life. I never thought it would be hard. And even the use of the word 'hard' makes me feel guilty, because I know how lucky I am to have two healthy children (they certainly didn't come easily – but those are stories for another day).

This book is a collection of letters written by incredible mothers from all over the globe to their children. Each letter is heartfelt, emotive, real, honest and full of passion and love. My gosh, there's a lot of love.

I hope this book inspires you to do the same and write a letter to your children, because if I've learnt one thing over the past month, it's that you'll always wish you said more to the ones you love.

> *"Let's start thinking about SUCCESS as being able to raise our children. Or having the COURAGE to slow down. Would that be so bad? I don't think so."*

This book is also a celebration of motherhood. While we live in a society in which motherhood is so often deeply undervalued (how many times have you heard a woman say "I'm just a mother" or had a moment at the end of the day with your kids when you almost feel invisible?), it's important to remember that there's no greater role in life than that of a parent. Nothing will ever be as significant. No job could ever compare.

Yet we're constantly encouraged to race back to work and smash as many career goals as possible. Career progression is lauded consistently as the marker of success in life. No wonder we can feel so lost when we first become mothers. We're constantly told to 'lean in', but what if we don't want to keep up with the frantic pace that society now expects of us?

What have I learnt? To lean in when I need to and lean out when I need to. Whether you're a full-time working mother, stay-at-home mother or running your own business, do what feels right for you, move at your own pace, ditch the mother guilt and don't worry about what anyone else thinks.

I love my work and it's a huge part of who I am; but I'm also aware of the great responsibility I was given when I became a mother and the importance of making sure my priorities are in place. Let's start thinking about success as being able to raise our children. Or having the courage to slow down. Would that be so bad? I don't think so.

I couldn't do it all, so I quit my dream job and went down a new path. It was unexpected, but motherhood is full of twists and turns. So don't forget to slow down from time to time. You don't have to do it all now. And you can do it your way.

Above all, this book is a reminder of just how important your role is as a mother. Cherish it. Celebrate it. Value it. And remember: you've got this, mama.

To my girls, Arabella and Lottie – you're the reason my life finally makes sense. You are my whole, entire world. Thank you for filling my heart with more love than I ever imagined possible. I adore you.

Georgie Abay

... AND WELCOME

Photographer Julie Adams *is the creative force behind the look of* The Grace Tales, *as well as being responsible for most of the wonderfully evocative portraits featured here in the pages of* Grace Mothers.

Photography really began for me as a little girl, when I was always looking through my mum's photo albums – I was so curious about people and moments in time. It wasn't long before I owned my own camera and was saving my pocket money to process my next roll of film.

The real fascination of photography for me has always been people – I like to capture that little bit of magic in everyone. Whether I have my camera with me at weekends to capture my kids or I'm shooting a fashion story or portrait, I'm always trying to create an image that brings a moment to life.

My passion for photography really evolved in my 20s, when I was working as a photographic assistant in London. I also studied photography in Florence, which ignited my love affair with Italy. The first breaks I got in my career were in London, where I shot for *The Independent* newspaper and *Marie Claire*, *Grazia* and *Red* magazines, before making the move to New York.

I have been working in photography for almost 20 years, and worked for such international publications as *Vogue* and *Harpers Bazaar*. I thank my lucky stars every day that I pursued my passion as my 'job'.

My greatest joy of all, though, has been in becoming a mum. My first daughter, Maddie, was born in New York, and soon after we made our way back to Sydney. Our second child, Vivienne, was born here. We moved to the idyllic Northern Beaches and it was during this time of navigating Australian family and working life that I had the great fortune of meeting Georgie Abay.

Well, what can I say... I met a kindred spirit.

Georgie had also pursued her love of publishing overseas and had her dream job at *Vogue* when we first met. She told me about her vision for a magazine-style website for mothers and in no time, we were madly shooting for the launch of *The Grace Tales*.

Georgie has such a clear vision. She's fearless, and no sooner does she think than she acts on her decisions. Having the opportunity to work with someone like this allows your confidence to grow and creativity to flow. She also has a twinkle in her eye – a quality I've always been drawn to – so, above all, working is fun!

The beauty of working on *The Grace Tales* has been the opportunity to meet so many inspiring women. Each story we shoot is so personal, as we are photographing women with their children, often in their own homes. To share these moments with people and their families is a privilege.

My most treasured moment working on *The Grace Tales* was when I first photographed Peta Murchison, who has since become a dear friend. Peta's little girl, Mia, stole my heart that day. She was suffering with Batten disease, a rare degenerative disorder that took her life at the age of nine. I was fortunate to have taken so many pictures with Mia, aware always of how precious every moment was. I'm honoured that Peta has shared her letter with us here; the images of Mia are, without doubt, my most cherished.

I am so proud to be part of *Grace Mothers* and thank all the other contributing photographers whose beautiful images also grace the pages of this book.

Grace Mothers is a beautiful collaboration of so many creative souls and I just want to say a heartfelt thank you to everyone who has made it so special.

Enjoy!

Julie Adams

TERESA PALMER

ACTRESS and CO-FOUNDER of YOUR ZEN LIFE and YOUR ZEN MAMA
Mother to BODHI and FOREST, stepmother to ISAAC

Australian actress Teresa Palmer had dreamt of being in movies since the age of eight, when she first watched Alfonso Cuarón's 1995 fantasy, A Little Princess. *Armed with determination and natural talent, she was always going to reach Hollywood-leading-lady stardom. While she made her debut in the film 2:37, she really made her mark in* Warm Bodies. *But an illustrious acting career is just the beginning: like her mother, a former nurse and missionary, Teresa is determined to give back, both through her philanthropic work and her online platforms,* Your Zen Life *and* Your Zen Mama.

Teresa comes from, as she puts it, "humble beginnings" in the Adelaide Hills, South Australia. Her parents divorced when she was three, and she and her mother, Paula, remain incredibly close. She met her husband, American actor/writer/director Mark Webber, on Twitter after she got in touch about a movie he'd made. They have two sons, Bodhi Rain and Forest Sage, and Teresa is also stepmother to Mark's son, Isaac. She is pregnant with her third child, a girl. The family divides its time between a home in LA and a four-hectare bush property in Adelaide.

Remarkably open and honest, Teresa communicates to fans through her YouTube *Tez Talks* videos – unfiltered and makeup-free. Beautiful both inside and out, she's an intriguing figure with an inspiring outlook on life.

To my beautiful children,

As I sit here and think about what I can share with you about life, my darlings, I realise my lessons and experiences can't be described adequately with words. But here goes...

Life is a series of feelings, emotions and choices to navigate. Each of you will journey life's path with your own reflections, desires and dreams, hitting bumps and growing wiser with each stumble. Each of you is unique, with your own voice and direction, and you are brave and bold enough to follow that path without fear of judgement. Follow the song of your heart and trust the knowing feeling in your tummy that guides you. This is your gravitational pull, that home feeling telling you you're exactly where you should be.

You've grown up travelling the world, so use what you've learnt about faith, culture and customs to cultivate curiosity and inform your decisions – that is where the magic lies. These adventures will enrich your life, change you, shape you and bring great perspective. More important than getting top grades! Find people who inspire you, spend time with them and learn from them. You can be anything you want to be – achieve anything!

You, my loves, have strong intuition, passionate spirits and genuine hope that the best things in life are accessible to everyone. You're dedicated to ensuring that the world suffers a little less. You care about animals and see them as beautiful, enriching beings that should be loved and nurtured, with the right to live as much as any other creature. When you willingly chose not to eat them, you convinced us, your parents, to follow. Your knowing and passion were so true and real. You are our teachers.

It's most important to use your goodness to help others. Being selfless is key: you can reach your goals while helping others do the same. Believe me, dreams are so much more fulfilling when shared. Look around you, find the lonely ones and give them your time – show them somebody cares. You cannot underestimate the power of kindness.

Please also be sure to extend this compassion to yourself. Cultivate self-love and don't spend a minute doubting yourself. It's ok to be human, with all your flaws, complexities and vulnerabilities. Those who embrace them are always the most interesting to me. Be gentle with others' hearts, but love fiercely! Importantly, be a good listener and a quiet observer. Having the social skills to walk into a room and 'read it' is essential, and being sensitive to other people's energy will make you a lovely friend, confidant and partner.

Try hard not to judge others, we're all just learning and doing our best. Not everyone will have your best interests at heart, but try not to be disappointed. If you know yourself, you will recognise when you need to establish loving boundaries. If you are led down a path that no longer serves you, head the other way. You have not failed; you have learnt something. The hard stuff is where all great lessons lie. If you can hold your head high no matter how big the crashing wave, you will understand the dark is not something to fear, it's an opportunity to go deeper, closer to the source of who you are. It won't be easy, but it will be good for you.

Your nanna taught me the importance of being playful. She played with me every day, let me be free, wild and *me*. Which is why I'm so playful, goofy and silly with you! She taught me that life is too short to worry about things we can't control. Focus on what you have, not what you don't. You will always have an abundance of happiness, adventure and people who love you. These are the seeds that have helped to form such loving, soulful, caring children.

Being your parent is, quite simply, my favourite thing in the world. It is *my* gravitational pull. We ride the waves together, connected as one. You continue to teach me about me and, although it's not always smooth, it is *always* full of colour – my absolute favourite, vibrant colours that make me so happy to be alive and even happier to be your mum. You make me laugh, swoon and love like I've never experienced before. You're my greatest joy – my home – and I'm so proud of you.

Love always, your Mama

"Being your parent is, quite simply, my FAVOURITE thing in the world. It is MY GRAVITATIONAL pull. You're my greatest joy – my HOME."

SAM BLOOM

COMPETITOR, SURVIVOR and SPEAKER
Mother to RUEBEN, NOAH and OLI

Sam Bloom's story is extraordinary – and, in many ways, it's only just beginning. The former nurse lives on Sydney's Northern Beaches with her three boys and photographer husband Cameron. Once an avid runner, swimmer and surfer, Sam's life changed dramatically in 2013 on a family holiday in Thailand. She fell through a rotten balcony railing and crashed six metres onto the concrete below. Her injuries left her paralysed from the chest down.

The early days after her accident were the darkest of Sam's life. Until Penguin arrived... "The guardian angel that saved my life was a baby bird," she says. Caring for Penguin gave Sam a purpose and, suddenly, her instincts as a nurse and mother were revived. "I found that helping someone else feel better was the best way to help myself feel better." Sam took up competitive paracanoeing, eventually placing 13th in the world and winning two Australian titles, before representing Australia at the 2015 World Titles in Italy. More recently, she was selected for the Australian Adaptive Surf team at the 2018 Stance International Surfing Association's World Adaptive Surfing Championship in San Diego. Meanwhile, Cameron had documented the family's experience through thousands of still images and videos, which led to a book, *Penguin Bloom*, written in collaboration with *New York Times*-bestselling Australian author Bradley Trevor Greive. Now an international bestseller, *Penguin Bloom* is being adapted into a feature film produced by Naomi Watts, who is also set to play the role of Sam.

To my three beautiful boys,

I'm so sorry. It wasn't supposed to be like this. I hate being paralysed. I hate not being able to stand, walk or run down to the beach and surf together like we used to. I hate the loss of feeling below my chest, as if two-thirds of my body was already dead. But what I hate most of all is I'm not who I once was, I'm not who I want to be, and I'm definitely not the mother you deserve.

We were all so happy before – I never could have imagined that life could be so perfect. Each of you was so special and unique and wonderful when you were born. Every minute together was pure joy: watching you open your eyes, staring all around, looking so adorably astonished as you made a thousand tiny discoveries before breakfast. I don't think anything could sound as lovely as hearing your children laugh, or holding on to their first almost-words.

I'm embarrassed to admit that I honestly thought I knew what true happiness was before I became a mum, but I was wrong. Your dad and I travelled the world together when we were young – free and fearless, and head over heels in love. Every day was an adventure that I never wanted to end. But through your eyes I saw a different world altogether, a place more precious than anything I can describe. The love you brought out of me felt like an enormous star growing inside my heart.

As each birthday came around, you did more and more to amaze me and make me proud. You drove me a little crazy, as well, riding that toy tractor in the house, marking all the floors and walls, but you also made all my motherhood dreams come true. And all I wanted, and still want, is for your childhood dreams to come true, as well.

But then I fell and couldn't get up. And because of my accident, instead of being a bright, guiding light in your lives, I feel terribly guilty that, for six years, I have cast a dark cloud over all of us; that I have ruined your childhood.

My instinct as your mother is to care for you, no matter what, and it breaks my heart that, instead, you are forced to care for me. Don't get me wrong, I am so grateful for the love and compassion you give me each day, but I still weep with frustration that our natural roles of parent and child have been so cruelly reversed.

I am so desperately sorry for the sadness that I brought home from hospital with me. I try to shed the feelings of bitterness and dread, I try to be positive, I try to stay strong and put on a brave face, God knows I do. But you boys see through me every time and I know it hurts you deeply to see me suffering. I know my tears make you feel just as sad and helpless as I do, and that is the very opposite of what I want.

My love for you and my hopes for your future transcend any personal battle I am facing. I want you to grow into strong, capable, loving young men. I want you to be happy and brave and true to who you are. You have made so many sacrifices for me, but now I want you to live boldly for me; I never want my wheelchair to be an anchor that holds you back from your best life.

As your mother, I want nothing so much as to cheer you on as you pursue your passions. Never give up on your dreams – promise me that you never will – and I promise you I will never give up trying to walk again.

Your love has sustained me through the worst moments of my life – you literally kept me alive. There were times when I felt myself falling into the darkness and I wanted the pain to stop so badly that I didn't want to wake up ever again. But just when I was losing my grip on life, your faces called me back to this world. I love you too much to ever leave you behind.

I want you to know how proud I am of each of you, and how excited I am to imagine what your talents will accomplish, who you will love and how far your dreams will take you. I have seen a great deal of this world and want you all to see even more.

Life is not always fair, but it is still beautiful if you will just lift up your head and open your eyes. Life is not always easy, but it is always bearable and, if you keep trying your best, you will eventually find yourself where you always wanted to be, doing what you always wanted to do.

When I first came home from hospital, I could never bear to look at the sea, believing I would never surf again. But today we are surfing together; it's not quite how it once was, but it still feels wonderful to ride the waves with you again. After flying home from Thailand, I never wanted to board another plane; the memories of how my horrific accident ruined our family holiday were utterly devastating. But a few years later, after countless hours of hard work in the gym and out on the water, I was on my way to Italy to compete in the Paracanoe World Championships and then to enjoy a wonderful family holiday with you in Rome. I may not be living as I want, but every year is a little better than the last; therefore, I am able to look forward to even better days ahead.

I hate what has happened to me, I'm not going to pretend otherwise, but there is much I love about my life and I'm not giving up. We have many adventures ahead of us, and your story is just beginning.

Nothing matters more to me than for you to know that I love you dearly and always will. Please don't put your life on hold for me. Do what makes you happy today, not tomorrow, as you never know what life has in store for you.

Don't take anything for granted. Be attentive to the details and do your best to appreciate the smallest pleasures in life, for they are the things you will miss most if you ever lose them. Trust me on that.

Be kind to everyone you meet, especially those who seem overwhelmed with anger or grief, because you cannot know what terrible burden they are struggling with. Your words and actions can make all the difference to them.

Please love and support each other, as you always have, for while you are amazing individuals, you are so much stronger together. I don't doubt that the three of you could do absolutely anything you put your minds to.

And whenever you see me or think of me, please remember me as I was, for that is how I want to feel, and that is how I want to be again one day. Know that I am trying my best to be the mother you deserve, fighting this daily battle with every ounce of strength I have. And when, on my bad days, you see me struggling, the anguish on my face is because I'm determined to make progress, not because I'm giving up. I will never give up on you, on myself or on us.

I miss Penguin and think about her a lot and how her arrival, like yours, seemed like a miracle. But while she gave us so much hope and joy and laughter, the truth is that these beautiful feelings were always inside us; we had just lost sight of them behind the fear and anger and heartbreak that consumed us. So I ask each of you to choose your friends carefully and to seek out the 'Penguins' in your life who can awaken the best aspects of your nature. Most of all, I encourage you to be a 'Penguin' for others.

I hate my wheelchair and all that it represents, but there is still so much in this life I am grateful for. I love your dad, I love our little home, the natural beauty and ocean at our doorstep, and the endless blue sky. I love the sound of songbirds – especially the magpies, obviously – and the warm, golden light of a summer afternoon, when we all sit outside on the front lawn.

But most of all, I love you and I am grateful that I didn't die, so that now I get to watch my three beautiful boys grow up. You are the best of everything this world has to offer, you are all my dreams come true at once, and I love you with all my heart.

x Mum

HEIDI MIDDLETON

FASHION DESIGNER / Mother to INDIA and ELKE

Heidi Middleton is a remarkable woman, an icon of Australian fashion, yet, when you meet her, she's one of the most humble.
Heidi co-founded one of Australia's most successful fashion labels, sass & bide, with her best friend, Sarah-Jane Clarke, in 1999. It began with customised jeans, which they sold at London's Portobello Market, and grew into a thriving global fashion empire.

In 2007, just after the birth of her second child, Elke, Heidi was diagnosed with breast cancer. She beat the cancer and now her positive energy is infectious. "Everything is richer and fuller and more wonderful after going through something like that, because you do have a feeling of mortality and feeling lucky to survive."
Heidi's first female inspiration was her mum, who taught her that love has to start with yourself before it can be given. Her mother would often remind Heidi that, no matter how bad her day, there were always people in worse circumstances. This upbringing inspired her not only as a fashion designer, but in her passionate support for women in need and the protection of children. (Heidi's parents were foster carers, so she saw firsthand how giving children the love they need can change their lives.)
In 2013, after she and Sarah-Jane sold their business, Heidi launched into the next chapter of her family's life. They moved to Paris, before falling in love with an historic property in the Medoc in south-west France, which required an extensive renovation. Heidi and the girls now divide their time between France and Sydney, and, in late 2018, Heidi set up fashion and art brand ARTCLUB.

India Grace and Elke Bay,

My beautiful girls, my beams of light. You know so well where you sit in my heart. You fill its corners and fuel its existence. I sometimes marvel at the replenishing well of love that keeps flowing for you... overflows. It knows no limit. It's a force in itself that cannot be stopped. It is both primal and ethereal.

The best moment of my day is waking you. Kissing your foreheads and cheeks, inhaling the scent of your sleepy skin and reminding you of my love for you. The birth of a new day brings both possibility and hope. It's the time of day to feel grateful.

I have always felt thankful for the foundation of love that my parents gave me in my childhood. It has been both an anchor and sail throughout my life – steadying and reassuring me in challenging times, and guiding me when I have felt uncertain. It gave me a strong sense of self, because I was immersed in love as a young girl. So, when life has presented me with adversity, I have managed to navigate forward with a level of trust, dignity and grace.

That foundation was always there for me. I tell you this because I yearn to instil that same sense of self-love and respect in the two of you. You are both uniquely beautiful, from the inside of your hearts to the outside of your skins. You are sensitive to others and understand that compassion is paramount in life. It's a fine balance to maintain the equilibrium between giving outwardly and nurturing self. I have always believed in living with love at the forefront. Love is the answer. Always choose love over hate.

Try not to be disappointed in life, but understand its complexity and beauty in equal measure. There will be hard times among the good, but if you can strive to see the blessings that are born out of hardship, then you will be able to move forward more easily.

Try to maintain a lightness of spirit. See the humour and quirks in the everyday. Life can feel heavy at times, and humour is a wonderful tonic. Put effort and meaning into all that you do. You don't have to be the best, but it's so important to work hard for things. You cannot control every detail and aspect of the world in which you live, but you do have the ability to control how you see the world and face certain situations. It is a gift in itself to realise this. Make it a habit to smile at people; not only does it feel good within, but the butterfly effect is limitless. Think how far that smile might travel and how many souls it will pass through, lifting each one a little on its journey.

Remember the strength, power and beauty of Nature. She will inspire, guide and comfort if you let her. Be aware of her magnificence and respect the vital role she plays in the world. Do what you can to preserve her. Life is a garden. If you water, nourish and nurture it; tend to it and pour effort and love into it, it will return in abundance. Think of your relationships and life projects in this way and you will enjoy the fruit that they bear. It is the fundamental law of Nature – generosity is rewarded. Be a giver.

I also want you to know that you were born out of love. Your father and I may not be together anymore, but our love was real and you are loved deeply by both of us. You will always be the jewels of our union, and for that I will always be grateful.

Thank you for choosing me to be your mum. It is by far my greatest honour.

Forever yours, Mama x

PANDORA SYKES

JOURNALIST, BROADCASTER and CONSULTANT / Mother to ZADIE

Since she first became Wardrobe Mistress columnist and fashion features editor of The Sunday Times Style *magazine, Pandora has charmed readers with her incisive musings and eclectic, independent approach to style, be it fashion or interior design. She is contributing editor at* Man Repeller *and* Elle *UK, a mentor on Peroni's incubator scheme for young designers and a panellist host and speaker. Her CV is a roll call of other esteemed publications, such as* The Guardian *and* Vogue *Australia, and sought-after brands, including Mango and Net-a-Porter. She also co-hosts the UK's top-rating women's culture podcast,* The High Low.

Pandora experienced an unexpected tidal wave of mother love when she gave birth. "I knew Zadie would change my life," she says. "As a naturally anxious person, I foresaw an anxiety that is yet to materialise. But in fact, I'm at my calmest and happiest when I'm with her. It's just this primal surge of She. Is. It." Happily for her many followers, she's been back at work since Zadie was five weeks old. "In hindsight, it was far too early to return, but it meant I was able to be both inside and outside of the 'baby bubble', which is probably quite a privilege of a straddle to make."

Dear Zadie,

I write this on your six-month birthday. (One day, not far from now, we'll stop celebrating your monthly milestones. We worked out recently that your father is 3939 months old. Suffice to say, they're no longer marked with banners.)

I'm sorry it's taken me so long to write to you. In any snatched moments of reflection, I find myself too distracted to write; rather, I am preoccupied trying to be both inside and outside of myself as a mother. How does it feel to parent you? What kind of parent am I, objectively? It's a wonder we introspects ever get out of our brains long enough to, well, make one of you.

Anyway, you're here. We managed. How incredibly lucky we are to have you. That said, this is a bit of a hard one for me to write. I've been so private about my experience of being not just a mother, but *your* mother – not with friends, but as a journalist – and I've just written a piece about why I'm being careful about what I share about you. But one day you'll want to know what you were like as a baby and what we were like then, and you might find it cool to see that I wrote you a letter, in a book. (Will books still exist when you're 21? God, I hope so.) And given how bad my memory is – I don't know what you did with it: stole it, ate it, burped it away – it's best to commit these memories to print.

You've always liked eating and sleeping – we are extremely lucky in that regard – and you were (everybody said it, so this isn't me being biased, promise) the most spectacularly gorgeous newborn. You came out so tanned and we couldn't stop cooing over your olive skin (your father is half-Portuguese), until your auntie, our midwife, told us that you were severely jaundiced. Now you're the colour of blancmange.

You were born in a freak March snowstorm at 3.17am – which is a neat parallel to your own mother, who was also born shortly after 3am, 30 years previously, in a freak March snowstorm. Just seven weeks later, we were in the garden in swimming costumes. That's global warming for you. (Will the world be powered by renewable energy by the time you read this? Here's hoping.)

We called you Zadie Grace Valentine and your pigletty grunts, pointed ballerina toes and non-stop gummy grins became your hallmark. Indeed, you smile so much that one of our friends asked if it was normal. I hope, like squillions of parents since the dawn of time, that you are not normal; that you are a one-off.

My relationship with you has transformed my relationship with my own mother. She already has two granddaughters, yet treats everything you do as new and exciting. Seeing her love you makes happiness bloom in me so quickly that sometimes I think I might faint.

She demands new pictures of you every day; inspects every part of you every time she sees you.

"I think her hair might be red, not blonde"... "Those eyelashes are her father's." Seeing her love you feels both entirely new and completely familiar. It reminds me viscerally of my own childhood.

We're lucky that we've had oodles of help with you, as I couldn't really take much time off work. Your father is the most charming, patient and happy man I could ever have as a co-parent. Working-mother's guilt is ubiquitous, but it took the benefit of hindsight (that beautiful thing), to note that maternity leave is as much about mental and physical recuperation as it is about nursing and bonding. The 'baby bubble' is not just a term; it is a physical and biological necessity. The upshot of all that is that I took August off to spend with you, something I want to try to do in all the years to come. As I write this, we are on our first proper family holiday. You've adapted so well to the European lifestyle and we've spent every minute of the past 11 days with you as a little pack of three. I write this from our balcony in Provence, as you snooze inside. If I strain, I can spy your bald head with its dusting of we-think-it's-blonde-but-could-be-brown hair and those little rosebud lips, clamped around a dummy.

So, what are my life goals for you, Zizi? (Your granny recently sent me a panicked text message that read: You know Zizi means 'willy' in French!?!?!?!?!?? Lucky we're not French then, I replied, unperturbed.)

I hope you have the courage to be truly yourself; that we arm you with the tools, the confidence and the freedom to be who you want to be and not what, however subconsciously, we want you to be. We hope you will be kind and thoughtful – because these are the qualities that your parents champion above all else – and that you will be content. Because success, no matter how immense, is nothing without contentment.

We hope you will be honest and carry yourself with inner conviction. I hope you have your father's patience and innate self-confidence: never has he walked into a room and wondered if he belongs. Above all, I hope you have the courage to be authentically and happily you – whoever that may be, Zadie Grace Tritton.

I don't want to be your best friend – I'm not going to be following you to the pubs and the clubs, trying to be 'cool mum' (a role I would inevitably fail at, incidentally). But I hope you'll be able to tell me things, even the things that scare you, even the things I might not want to hear. *Especially* those things.

So, happy six months, baby girl.

I love you, I love you, I *love* you. x

STACIE HESS

PHOTOGRAPHER, MODEL and JEWELLERY DESIGNER
Mother to AMELIA

"People in Hawaii don't live to work, they work to live. There isn't that need for a 'career' like we have here in LA," says Stacie Hess. Born in Hawaii, she grew up in a culture where everything is about family.
"Having that Hawaiian upbringing around family has really shaped my approach to motherhood, my career, my life and my relationships."

Stacie started modelling when she was 11 years old and landed her first acting gig – as one of the original Disney movie girls – when she was 14. A self-taught photographer, she first picked up a camera about five years ago. Her namesake jewellery line is a collection of exquisite heirloom pieces that are handmade in wax, then cast in 14k or 22k gold, each designed to be passed down from one generation to the next.

Amelia,

My baby girl.

The world is a tough, yet beautiful place. At the moment, you're nine, and I can say that you're already learning that, and becoming such a strong and passionate soul.

In my 34 years on this Earth, I've lived through a lot, messed up a lot and learnt and grown a ton from all of it. It's made me into the woman I am now and I want to share with you some of what I've learnt thus far:

Explore. Explore your city. Explore the world. Get out and move. Travel as much as possible – the experience you gather and tough spots you will need to get yourself out of will enrich your entire being. Go out and see how the rest of the world lives. Explore different cultures and food. Food! Try all of it. Be adventurous. Take buses and trains and walk and hike and jump on that last-minute flight. I started travelling much too late and my wish for you is that you continue to get out and explore – with friends, on your own, with me.

Don't be afraid to screw up; we all do. Nobody's perfect (except maybe Bunny...). As long as you learn from your mistakes and do better the next time, it's not the end of the world (but it *could* be the end of the world, so be safe!).

Learn to say you're sorry. Be humble and admit when you've messed up. Learn from that and be better.

Love yourself before you attempt to love anyone else. The relationship you have with *you* will be the most important relationship you ever have. You need to love and understand all the parts that make you *you*. The physical aspects: it's ok to be in love with your hair and to have your two favourite little beauty marks. Love your body and your physical features – I *love* that you love yourself right now. Don't be hard on yourself in the future as your body changes. Our bodies are beautiful and everchanging through the different stages of our lives. We give birth to precious little beings like you and bounce right back to do it over and over again.

Remember, though, that your physical beauty is just a mirror to your internal beauty. Be a good person. Always think of others and don't speak badly of your friends. Don't be judgemental, because the time will come when you won't appreciate being judged, either. Love what a kind and thoughtful person you are. Know that you will never intentionally do harm to others. Know that you are good.

When you *do* fall in love, make sure it's a fairytale-ending kind of love; not a 'princess being rescued by a prince' kind of ending, but 'happily ever after'. Never settle for less happiness than you know you deserve. At nine years old, you can already see epic gestures and you know what love looks like. Remember those stories and moments you've already wished for yourself. I also wish them for you.

I hope you work your butt off to create the life you want. Never expect anyone else to take care of you. Work hard. Believe in yourself. You are capable. You are smart. You are strong. When you fall, get off the floor and get right back into it. We all fall; that's life.

But whatever you do in this life, you are my baby, my greatest accomplishment, my best friend. You are my travelling partner, my soulmate, my everything. I will always be there to pick you up when you've fallen, when you've messed up; to talk to you when you need help with friends and boys, and to make you laugh when you're upset. Because I love you – yes, even when I'm mad.

Beyond infinity, Mommy

SIBELLA COURT

INTERIOR DESIGNER, STYLIST and AUTHOR / Mother to SILVER

Sibella Court is one of Australia's most respected interior and product designers and stylists, an author (six books in nine years – her latest, published in 2018, is Imaginarium*), television presenter and owner of design studio and treasure-trove homewares store The Society Inc. She's also one of those people who you imagine has trouble deciding what to list under 'occupation' on the form at passport control, as she travels the world for her various roles during much of the year.*

At age 41, she became a mother to her daughter, Silver. It's unbelievable how much she fits into her life and still manages to remain cool, calm and collected, though Sibella freely admits to regularly feeling overwhelmed. "Who doesn't? But every day is different. I feel overwhelmed, insecure, confident, on top of the world, and that's all in one day, isn't it?! And then you throw a kid into the mix!" she laughs.

Dear Silver,

Sitting on the couch last night with your dad, we reminisced over a picture of you when you were a baby. Your foot was so tiny, barely the size of his thumb. That time after you were born was so precious. We spent a while at our beautiful beach shack in Byron Bay, where I'd sit on the deck at nighttime, breastfeeding and looking out to the moon.

Creativity runs in our family. As a child, my creativity began with a fascination with collecting and displaying beautiful things: one of my earliest collections was of assorted beads and ribbons organised into similar colours and styles. I remember, from the age of two, collecting a particular type of kelp shell that has shades of pink with zigzags on it. Your great-grandparents lived on Smiths Lake, which shares a sandbank with the ocean, where I would search up and down the shoreline all day seeking out the shells, then arranging them in small glass jars.

Over the past year, you've become so creative and crafty, which has been so lovely for me, because art is such a big part of my life. It's a joy to watch you beachcombing and doing all the things I love doing.

When you first arrived, it was quite the juggle. I was relaxing into my new role of mother while running a company and shooting a TV show for the ABC called *Restoration Australia*. I recommenced work when you were six weeks old and carried you around with me in a sling while I was filming. You travelled around Australia and the world with me, and were such a well-travelled Gypsy before you reached your second birthday. Your Papa often accompanied us to look after you on my trips to rural Australia, and you became the best of friends.

Work has always been such a joy for me. I've loved every single day of my career, whether it's been challenging or smooth sailing. When you spend so much time working, making sure you are passionate about what you do is one of the most important lessons in life. Pick something you love and follow your dreams. You don't have to do it the way other people do it. Have the confidence to think outside the box.

I started my own company at the age of 21. It just happened very organically, and as someone who didn't have a program or systems in place, I very much flew by the seat of my pants. Your grandfather was a builder who ran his business from home, so I watched him work and saw that it was possible. Recently, though, your dad

started working for the company and has helped put systems in place! When I started, there was no hesitation or thinking I was being courageous; I just did it.

I endeavour to be an available mum to you. And fun, although your dad says I'm probably too much fun! But most importantly, available for you, so you can always be open with me, no matter what you're going through. I hope I'm always a sounding board throughout your life.

I dreamt about your grandmother last night. She was crouching down against a wall waiting for you to see her. I woke up sobbing, but they were happy tears. You talk about your Nanny Dee often, even though she died years before you were born. When I was living in New York, she sent me a book by Jeanette Winterson called *Lighthousekeeping*. The opening sentence is: 'My mother called me Silver. I was born part precious metal part pirate.' Your grandmother suggested that this would be a perfect name for my first baby. And it is. Your middle name is in honour of her Gypsy spirit.

She was such an inspiration to me and someone who really followed her dreams. She had a few chapters in her life and taught me that, regardless of the chapter you're in, there are more to come.

I love that idea, because if I ever feel like I want to change something, I think of it as starting a new chapter. My mum always said that everything is a phase. We all go through phases, and it doesn't matter if it's a couple of weeks or a decade, life will keep shifting into new phases.

It's not always a straight path, but there's a lot of adventure, fun and enjoyment that can come through the ebb and flow of life. Think of life as a lovely moving journey, like a beautiful river through a landscape with bends and curves. Expect the unexpected and as much as you put into it, you'll get out of it. There's something really lovely about wondering what's going to happen next.

I never knew if I'd become a mother. Now I am one, I couldn't imagine my life differently. When I was pregnant, I hoped we'd become really good friends, and we have. We have each other forever.

You have absolutely charmed me. Right now, you're my little cub, who's going to follow me around until you're ready to go out on your own. I hope you'll come back time and time again. I often tell you that we will be best friends forever.

Love, Mum

> "*I hoped we'd become really GOOD FRIENDS, and we have.*"

ANINE BING

FOUNDER and CHIEF CREATIVE OFFICER of ANINE BING
Mother to BIANCA and BENJAMIN

*LA-based designer and mother of two Anine Bing has lived many lives.
Born in Denmark and raised in a small town in Sweden, she was a model at
15, then a singer/songwriter, before she transformed her blog into a global
womenswear empire, building her eponymous brand via social media.
"I have done so many things in my life and worn a lot of different hats," she
says. "I would say that in each one I was able to find happiness and that makes
all of them successes to me. Every time we open a new store, that joy of sharing
my passion with the world feels like another win. But also sometimes success
just means getting home with enough time to hang out with my kids."*

Here, in her elegant West Coast home, with her husband, Nicolai, and their two children,
Bianca and Benjamin, is where Anine now feels most content.
"I have always wanted to be a mom, ever since I was a little girl, and it has been more
than I ever dreamed of," she says. "It has made my life so full. It has taught me how
to prioritise and how to love more than I thought I could. My kids remind me of what's
important and it means so much to see them succeed... The happiest moments are simple,
and they make every tough moment worth it." Here, Anine pens a letter to Bianca.

"I only ask three things: that you always BELIEVE in yourself... that you stay OPEN-MINDED and willing to grow... that you THROW FEAR OUT of the window."

To my daughter,

The other day, I was sitting at your karate class and you were kicking like I've never seen a kid kick before. You kicked higher than all the boys in that class. You watched with a careful eye and then went after what you wanted with full force. In these moments, I know you have so much power and are dedicated to what you want. This is why you are special.

I know you probably think I'm saying all this because I'm your mother, and that's true. I'll always love you more than most, but I believe, my sweet girl, that you are special. Special because you are brave, funny and confident; but also special because you are a woman. I remember the first day you were born. We stayed up all night just looking into each other's eyes. We had an instant connection, my little girl with the huge brown eyes.

Being a mom has changed me, and I have you to thank for that. Your scope of lessons is wide. You have made me a professional juggler, teaching me how to get a million things done in no time, when before you, one errand could take me the whole day.

You have taught me how to laugh; and not just a quick giggle, but to really laugh and enjoy myself during life's funny moments. You have taught me how to cut away all the nonsense. There are only 24 hours in the day and, with you, I have learnt how to spend them right – reading you bedtime stories, sharing a croissant with you, or singing the songs my mom used to sing with you. Besides being a built-in alarm clock for my mornings, you have taught me how to prioritise my time and choose what's important – you and Benjamin always, work emails only sometimes.

I'll be the first to admit I don't have it all figured out. I want to set an example for you: that following your dreams is worth it, that hard work is worth it. But this makes me a working mom, which means that sometimes I can't tie everything up with a bow at the end of the day. I would love to be able to cook you and Benjamin great dinners every night. I know what usually ends up happening is take-out and some extra cuddles to make up for it. I dream about being the mom who has healthy food prepared on a daily basis, but I also dream about setting realistic expectations for you and being a role model. So here's a piece of advice: it's ok if you can't do it all.

Sometimes you will feel like you aren't enough. As a woman, I feel like I want to be everywhere and do my best everywhere, and it's not always possible. My lesson to you, little one, is that you should never be so hard on yourself. Being a woman is hard work! Focus on one thing at a time. You won't be able to do everything and that's ok. Take care of yourself.

I have learnt through my trials that picking your priorities is the key to being happy and, while I might not always have a hand-tossed salad for you on the table, I will always be ready with a hug, a laugh, or an ear to listen. Choose the things that fill your soul and do those things fully, instead of doing a million things half-assed. Trust me on this one.

A lot of parents have dreams and hopes for their kids; for you, I only ask three things:

That you always believe in yourself. I don't care if you get into Harvard or run your own company. I want you to live your life without pressure, but always with purpose. Travel the world and figure out who you are and who you want to be. Your only demand of yourself should be to follow your heart. By doing this, you will find your people, your happiness and yourself.

That you always stay open-minded and willing to grow. I look at you, seven years old as I write this, and you are so much more than a seven-year-old should ever be. You have the best sense of humour and are so creative – always coming up with little drawings of designs you think I should add to collections. You're an old soul, and so caring and sweet to everyone around you. Don't lose that. Stay open to all kinds of people, lift other women up and keep running wild with your imagination. Stay smart and intuitive by keeping your eyes open. Say yes to things that scare you, but say no to things you don't have time for. It's important to remember it's ok to take chances, but it's also ok to say no when you need to.

That you throw fear out of the window. If you live in fear, you will never win. I would never have come this far with my business if I wasn't willing to try and maybe fail. Don't worry so much; everything will be ok. I guess I always followed my dreams, but I also always worried along the way. So I hope you will be more present and not worry as much about the future. It is yours and you are ready to take it.

The best gift my mom gave me was letting me be me. I can write this letter, but only you can be in charge of writing your story. So just be, and you will conquer the world.

Love you always, Mommy

GRETCHEN CARLSON

JOURNALIST, AUTHOR and ADVOCATE
Mother to KAIA and CHRISTIAN

She's the American TV news veteran who paved the way for the #MeToo movement. Following Gretchen's sexual harassment claims in 2016, Roger Ailes, CEO and chairman of Fox News, was forced to step down and she received a reported $20 million settlement. Named one of Time's '100 Most Influential People in the World', *Gretchen has written* two New York Times *bestsellers,* Be Fierce *and* Getting Real.

"I was always sleep-deprived working the early-morning shift, and I'm not a napper," she says. "But it was great when the kids were little, because I went to work for four hours before they woke up and was home by noon when they were home from preschool, so they never missed me! I have always been a busy person, so fitting in kids with work was hard, but not incredibly overwhelming."

Dear Kaia and Christian,

My parents raised me with discipline. Every night when she put me to bed, my mother would tell me, "You know, Gretchen, you can be anything you want to be in this world. God has given you many talents and He expects you to use them."

My mother was my rock and foundation. She taught me how to be driven and goal-oriented, how to persevere in the face of anything and to never, ever give up. My father taught me grace, humility, patience, how to listen and certainly to have a sense of humour. These are all lessons and values I am now passing on to you.

I *always* wanted to be a mom! I remember being in the hospital with pneumonia when I was a little girl – maybe five or six – and my room had a window into the newborn room. I continually asked the nurse if she could lift me up to see all the babies!

As hard a worker as I have always been, I always knew I wanted children. I still look at you each night and see your cherub faces and know how lucky I am. You are a great joy and accomplishment in my life. No matter what, after a long or hard day, everything becomes more relevant the minute I see you.

Christian, you, especially, make me laugh. You have a great sense of humour and wake up almost every morning with a smile on your face and a great attitude! Recently, you looked at me and said, "Mom, you are just my scrumptious shrimp!" (I'm not tall!)

Kaia, you are so organised and have so much tenacity in wanting to do well. You are such a hard worker and so giving to others. But remember also to stop every once in a while and take time to relax and be proud of yourself.

I want to be the kind of mom who is present! I believe women are made to feel guilty about being away from their kids if they happen to work. I have never felt any guilt! I'm a better mom because I *do* work and I feel like I'm providing a great roadmap for when you grow up and pursue your dreams. While I'm a hands-on mom, I also know how important it is to allow you to be in charge of your lives and learn how to fail in order to succeed.

You know that your parents are all about effort, whatever we are attempting to do. With schoolwork, we expect effort and hope for good grades, but it's the time and commitment that are important.

I put 100 per cent effort into everything. When you put time into something, you realise very early on that you get better at it, and that builds self-confidence and self-esteem. A strong work ethic is something no one can ever take away from you, no matter how hard they try.

Our family mantra is that we never, ever give up. Simply because you're losing in a basketball game or at Monopoly, you don't give up just because you don't want to lose. You have to finish what you start!

I believe that you can only truly appreciate success when you fail. Overcoming failure teaches you resilience, even during hard times. I often tell you what happened to me one day in 10th grade. In one day, I lost the class

president election, didn't make the Oklahoma play ensemble, and didn't make a singing and dancing group I auditioned for. It was a tough day. My grandfather then asked me if I knew how many times it had taken for Thomas Edison to invent the light bulb. He told me that Edison had had more than 2000 failures first!

Being from Minnesota, I was raised to value every dollar and every day. I am trying to instil the same values in you, especially living in the New York City area, where it can be hard to not get caught up in material things.

When I jumped off the cliff all by myself to bring a sexual harassment lawsuit against my boss at Fox News, there were no #MeToo movement or Time's Up pins. It was just me, taking on one of the most powerful men in the world. And you were my paramount concern. How would you fare? How would you be treated? Would you be ok?

Turns out I underestimated you. It was the first day of school and I was really nervous. But Kaia, you came home and said, "Mom, a lot of people asked me about you today and what happened to you over the summer – and, Mommy, I was so proud to say you were my mom."

A couple of weeks later, when a few fellow students had been making your life rough and you hadn't found the courage to stand up to them, you came home and said, "Mommy, today I finally dug deep to do what I needed to do. I told that one this and this one that. And Mommy, I did it because I saw you do it!"

A year later, I was at a town hall on CNN, talking about harassment. Christian, when I came home, you said, "Mommy, was that statistic on TV true? That once every 73 seconds, a woman is harassed or assaulted in our country?" I replied, "Yes, I'm so sorry to tell you that is true." You looked at me and said, "Mommy, I want to be a part of fixing that."

Giving the gift of courage happens one person at a time. And even if I felt I had given it only to you both, it would be enough. But I've found out that giving the gift of courage is contagious, and look where we are today – in a cultural revolution, with women finally being believed and the men who've harassed them being held accountable.

I am a person of faith, and that is what gives me strength in difficult times. And I also feel it's important to give you the foundation of faith in your lives, so when you become adults, you can choose your own paths. I believe that if you realise you aren't alone in the world when you're feeling lonely or anxious, faith can be a huge support system.

Seeing what you will become – in college and careers, with marriage and your own children – fills me with hope. I come from a very close family and my grandparents meant everything to me, so I hope I can be the same for your children.

Every day you give me hope that tomorrow will be a better place for everyone. You are the lights of my life and I will cherish you forever.

Love, Mom

JANICE PETERSEN

SBS WORLD NEWS PRESENTER and JOURNALIST
Mother to ODESSA and ARKIE

There are two things you notice when you first walk into the charming terrace home of Janice Petersen and her husband, Julian Hamilton (one half of electronic band The Presets). First, her refined intelligence and second, her fabulous sense of style. Meet her two girls, Odessa and Arkie, and you'll see they've inherited their mother's fantastic eye for fashion. In fact, we spent the first half hour of our photo shoot pulling out leopard print faux fur coats, leather jackets, Dr. Martens boots and more from their closet.

Born in Sydney to South African parents, Janice grew up on the New South Wales Central Coast and was a former national sprinter and high jumper, before going on to work for the ABC. Last year marked a decade with the SBS TV network, where she is a journalist and co-anchor of the evening news bulletin. Passionate about her work, Janice hopes her children are "learning that the satisfaction and independence women get from their work can make them happier people and therefore better mums".

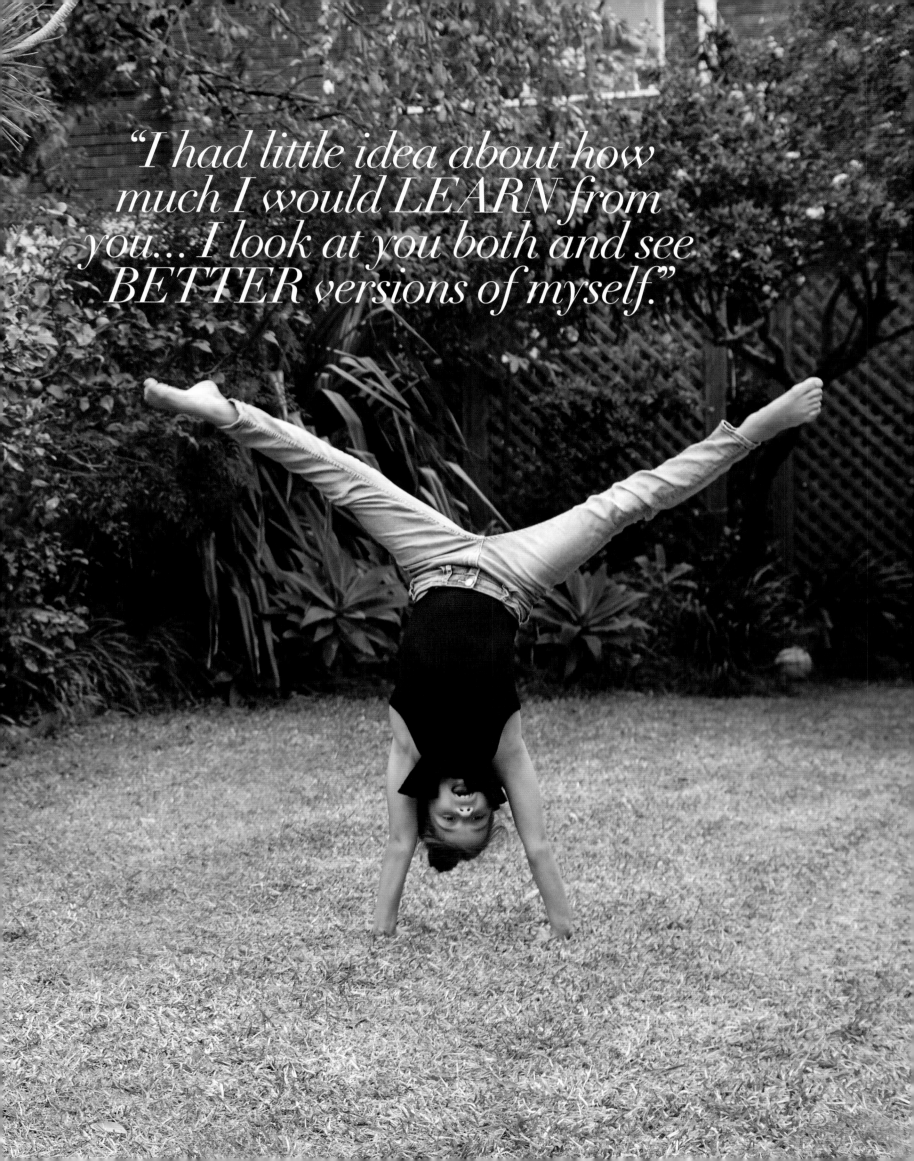

"I had little idea about how much I would LEARN from you... I look at you both and see BETTER versions of myself."

Dearest Odessa and Arkie,

I'm lucky enough to have had these past years, shared with Daddy, to teach, nurture and guide you before you head out into the world on your own. When that happens, I'll still be here. I will always love you.

You are both so different in many ways, but then also so alike.

Arkie, your self-awareness was brought into stark relief recently, when you were only four years old. I was trying to share some past memories with you, but said dismissively, "You wouldn't remember because you weren't born yet."

Your response rendered me speechless. "I was floating around the universe, hunting for parents."

You are a remarkable kid. You have such a different way of thinking and our whole family is awestruck by the sage wisdom that sprouts from your one-liners. You believe that you control your fate and have done so even before you came to be. Who are we to argue? Thanks for picking me and Dad to be your parents while you were traversing the galaxy.

Odessa, you are bottled sunshine. Your laughter is much like you: irrepressible. I get more pleasure from your unbridled, raucous cackle than any joke, ever. My great hope is that no one and nothing will ever dull your shine. I'd like to think that in some small way your dad and I have given you the confidence to laugh wildly from your guts with no inhibitions, but I suspect you were simply born that way.

When I walked into your room when both of you were babies, I would smell you sometimes before I saw you. That very special scent of 'you' triggered a wave of love that would radiate from my head, my heart and belly, and swirl all around me. You somehow created a magic 'love fertiliser' that made my heart grow.

It's hard to believe it still happens, but it does. Sometimes I just stare at you when you're sleeping. Time stops. I swear I forget to breathe.

The two of you are simply divine.

I love seeing the care you have for one other. Sometimes it's a gentle resting of your hand on your sister's shoulder, or touching her hair. Or the gentle holding of the cheeks when bestowing the 'good morning' kiss. Both of you do it unknowingly and it's a healing salve for whatever the day is about to throw at us.

Sometimes my heart hurts when I drop you both off at school, much like it did during the daycare years. It hurts because I feel like I say goodbye more than I say hello. I don't get to do the school pick-ups because of my job. I spend a lot of time working, but I feel that it makes me love you more. I know that you love what I do, too, and are fascinated by my job as a journalist and newsreader.

I hope that you are learning that the satisfaction and independence women get from their work can make them happier people and therefore better mums. Apparently women *can* have it all; just not all at once.

I saw my beautiful parents dedicate themselves to work, but that was never at the expense of their love for me and my brother. It warms my heart to see that you are now experiencing their incredible love, too.

I thought as a mother I'd have to give a lot to you and your sister. It is an important and joyous part of being a mum, but I had very little idea about how much I would learn from you two.

I look at both of you and see better versions of myself. Each generation feels that they should improve on the previous one. I can see from you both that this has already happened.

Thanks, my darling Dessi and Arks, for being so easy to love.

Much love, Mama

CAROLYN ASOME

WRITER / Mother to DECCA, ILSE and UDO

"Motherhood has taught me to ditch worry, guilt and stress, because they are incredibly time-wasting and don't achieve anything. And to put yourself first, because days are so relentless that if you don't, the whole pack of cards crumbles... And how your heart just grows with each child that comes along."

A former fashion editor for the *The Times*, London-based Carolyn Asome is now a freelance contributor to *The Times*, *The Telegraph* and British *Vogue*. She is also the author of two books for *Vogue* – *Essentials: Handbag*s and *Vogue on Jean Paul Gaultier*. "I love the variety of this new freelance chapter," says Carolyn. "And that I spend most of my time interviewing people who are hugely passionate about what they do, and how that energy rubs off."

Darling Decca, Ilse and Udo,

I never did get round to starting your baby journals. You know that as a full-time working mother, I was never one to feel 'mum guilt', but not filling them in sometimes niggled. So here I am making amends. Perhaps more useful than recording a six-month-old's milestones – well, we all learn to walk and talk, eventually – is for me to pass on the life maxims I try to live by and the lessons I've learnt the hard way.

Having a strong sense of self has helped me immeasurably – that is, knowing one's mind, values and ideals, and sticking to them. Respect and love yourself, too, because in the end, you are all you really have. No one is in charge of your happiness except you, whatever curveballs life hurls your way.

I've always thought there should be compulsory school exams in emotional intelligence. It's possibly the single most useful skill to help you thrive in life and the workplace. Learning to be self-aware and reading how you fit into a situation are far more important than any career service at university will ever impress on you. And don't underestimate how far being charming will take you in life.

I've learnt not to put limits on myself or over-think things. You don't truly know what you are capable of until you've tried it.

Equally motivating on a sluggish day:
"What would you do if you weren't afraid?"
"What if I fall?"
"Oh, but darling, what if you fly?"

This will ultimately mean stepping out of your comfort zone, which is an entirely good thing. So, too, is learning to go with the flow. This is otherwise known as accepting and acknowledging that life is Shakespearean and that shit happens. Things sometimes don't pan out as you wish, no matter how organised you are, so learn to let go.

Learn to be 'light', too, because when there's a light hand on the tiller (controlled, calm and confident), everything runs more smoothly; everything just *is* better.

Remember, too, that failing is essential for growing and learning. Mistakes are your greatest lessons, so embrace them. This will also encourage you to be emotionally resilient. Don't care too much about what others think and remember to see beyond the end of your nose. There is nearly always a rational explanation for why someone hasn't got back to you. Are they having a bad time? Has their dog just died? Everyone has their own agenda.

When it comes to work, there's an old Chinese proverb: 'Find a job you like and you will never work a day in your life.' I was lucky to find that job. Also, it's ok if school isn't great. I enjoy 'life' much more than I enjoyed school.

Choose the right life partner – *especially* if you want children. It is one of the most important decisions you will ever make, so choose wisely. Find someone who is sure enough of themselves to allow you to be the person *you* want to be.

Now, I love you all very much, but looking after small babies can be incredibly isolating, not to mention really bloody boring. Make choices that work for you, and to hell with what everyone else is doing. For me, that meant working full-time, rarely doing pick-ups and not 'seeing' the mess at home. Having that career allowed me to live in the present, both at home and at work.

I very much hope that your parenting landscape will have changed by the time you get there, because in 2019, it sucks. It never ceases to amaze me how many working-mother friends – bright, educated, go-getting, non-doormat women, married to smart, accomplished, understanding, reasonable men – still end up doing it all.

I sometimes feel women lose perspective when they roll their eyes, moan and tell me it's just easier when they do it themselves. Really? Better for whom, exactly? Is there really a 'bad' way of loading the dishwasher? No one way is better. Remember, most men won't lift a finger if women continue to be so controlling. Often it's women, hard-wired to be perfectionists (so dull!), who are as much to blame. Men-bashing is an impediment to your sanity, so stop it this instant.

It's being bogged down in the never-ending daily minutiae and juggling a career that often prevents women from having the head space to go and achieve great things. It is anathema for most women, but I hope they learn how important it is to put themselves first. So many have bought into the crap idea that they have to sacrifice everything they are and put themselves last in order to be a good mother, wife, daughter or friend. Far from being selfish, when you put yourself first, you are taking responsibility for yourself, which has always struck me as quite a sensible thing to do. When you put yourself first, *everything* in your life benefits.

Learning to ditch worry, guilt and stress unless something really bad happens has been an immense time-saver. It is also guaranteed to leave you with a deep sense of calm. A trip to Accident & Emergency is my benchmark here; not that I forgot to pack the waterproofs for the Year 4 canoeing trip.

Three things I would tell my 17-year-old self: buy less, buy better, even when you're a teenager with no budget. The things you worry about are rarely the things that happen. Be kind, because I believe in karma 200 per cent.

Finally, life is about people, not stuff. No one lay on their death bed wishing their house had been tidier. So I'll finish with the following from Esther Perel:

The quality of your life ultimately depends on the quality of your relationships. Not on your achievements, not on how smart you are, not on how rich you are, but on the quality of your relationships, which are basically a reflection of your sense of decency, your ability to think of others, your generosity... It will be about how you treated the people around you and how you made them feel.

Love from Mummy

CALGARY AVANSINO

WELLBEING EXPERT and AUTHOR
Mother to AVA, MARGOT and REMY

When it comes to health and wellbeing, the glamorous former British Vogue *contributing editor, author of cookbook* Keep It Real, *and mother of three knows a thing or two about achieving balance after babies. Calgary is also refreshingly honest about the fact that there's no magic bullet to achieving the elusive balance we're all striving for...*

"I wish there was! I try to give my all to whatever I'm doing, so when I'm working, I'm focusing on that, and when I'm Mummy, then I focus on my children. It is not always easy... But I really do try to separate the two. I think the stress hits you when you can't keep the two separate – like when homework needs to get done and so does a conference call. I hate those moments! But it's also great for my girls to see what working means and how to navigate it all as gracefully as possible," she says.

Dear Ava, Margot and Remy,

Don't waste a moment of this spectacular life! You could have been a million other DNA sequences, but you're not. You're magically you – exactly as you are meant to be, and one of your most important jobs is to maintain a deep connection to that 'you-ness' . You were profoundly wanted and are intensely cherished just as you are. Hold that belief tight.

Before I carried you, I didn't have an emotional connection with the notion of unconditional love. It's still not something I can define or explain rationally, but it's something I *feel* unequivocally. It washes over me every day, often at the most unexpected times.

You came from me and we are tied inextricably; but it's not about me. The beauty is your independence and you forging your own unique space in this world. I am simply here to listen, to gently guide, to support and to throw love in your direction at every opportunity.

It's usually not until the end of our lives that we truly understand the fragility and velocity of our time here, but if I were to pass on any advice from the years I have lived it would be this:

• Try not to wish away tough times, cold days or tedious hours. The pace of life is fast enough, so attempt to find presence in everyday moments.

• Love wildly with your whole heart – embrace the bruises and continue to be amazed by love's resilience.

• Laugh as often as you can, cry whenever you need to and turn up the music and dance. Dance alone, dance with others, dance in private, dance in public – just dance. Rein in your self-consciousness and let your soul move.

• Focus on moving forward; don't let past experiences, failures or negative memories paralyse you. Instead, use them as opportunities to practise perseverance and propel yourself in a positive direction.

• You're going to have failures and setbacks – they are life's guaranteed gift with purchase. The sooner you accept the waves of peacefulness and turbulence, the more equilibrium you'll feel navigating the human experience.

• Drop perfection from the equation – it will only torture you.

• Smile at yourself in the mirror at least once a day. You are special, valued and treasured.

• Remember to tell your mom you love her, too :)

Love and hugs, Mommy

ELLE HALLIWELL

JOURNALIST and AUTHOR / Mother to TOR

Two years ago, Sydney-based Elle Halliwell discovered she was pregnant. It should have been the happiest moment of her life, yet two days before that, she had been diagnosed with chronic myeloid leukaemia (CML), a rare blood cancer. "Knowing my illness had been discovered in its early stages, we decided to speak to world expert in CML, Timothy Hughes at South Australia's SAHMRI, who gave us the confidence to continue with the pregnancy," she recalls.

In December of 2016, Elle and her husband, Nick, were blessed with a beautiful son. "Meeting Tor for the first time was surreal... There was also an incredible sense of relief for me, knowing he was healthy, despite the challenges we had both overcome since he was conceived."

Elle's first book, *A Mother's Choice*, was published last year. "I got the best outcome. I have a cancer treatment that is working and I have an adorable healthy son. I feel like the luckiest person on earth."

Dear Tor,

It's nice to meet you. To *really* meet you. In the first few months after you were born, there wasn't much in the way of effective communication between us. You cried, I fed you. You cried again, I rocked you. You cried a little more, I changed you. You cried even more, and then I cried, too.

There were lots of tears in those first few months. You were adjusting to a big, scary new world, full of hunger, confusion and the presence of a large grey and white hairy being with a penchant for sniffing your hair (who you would later come to know as 'Meow').

I was also adjusting to my own terrifying new world, one of confusion (Is that poo normal?), worry (Oh my god the bath was too hot!) and exhaustion – and that was just the whole motherhood bit.

I also had my own demons to battle, which offered a different set of mental and physical challenges. You see, a few days before you graced your dad and me with your presence via the small window on a pregnancy test, I'd been diagnosed with leukaemia. So, when I began the long, slow process of healing myself of this dreaded disease after your birth, exhaustion, fatigue, bone pain and skin problems often competed for my attention. There were days when I felt completely hopeless and overwhelmed, but we got through it and, as the fog lifted, our bond grew stronger.

There are days when you light up my soul like Sydney Harbour on New Year's Eve. Other days, you test me in more ways than I ever thought possible. It doesn't take much to bring me back into joy, though: a butterfly kiss, a downcast pout, a heartfelt yet poorly articulated "Sowwy". I want to store those moments, pack them tightly in my heart where they can never spoil or fade.

Some days, I'm frozen in grief over what may have been had I made a different choice. I can't imagine a life without your sweet giggles, sandy curls and gentle hugs. Perhaps that's why some mornings I rise before the sun and pad silently into your room to watch you dream, just to savour a few more moments of the day with you.

> *"I bristle when I hear people call YOU a 'miracle child'. Yes, you're MY MIRACLE, undoubtedly, but so is EVERY mother's child."*

You look like a miniature replica of your father. You have his cerulean blue eyes, milky skin and the same small dimple on your left cheek. You share the same cheeky disposition and love of socialising, too. I'm glad you're already such a people person; the days I have to wave goodbye at daycare and head to work seem much harder for me than for you.

It's not easy for us mums these days. Sure, we have so many conveniences (hello online shopping, organic frozen baby food and babysitting apps!) as well as the freedom to live out our dreams. But what we also have is a crippling pressure to do everything and be everything to everyone.

We're caregivers, CEOs, business owners, cleaners, cooks, counsellors, taxis, wives and partners, and that's only a few of the roles today's women have to take on each day.

Mums truly are amazing creatures. I hope that when you grow up, you have an appreciation for the awesomeness of women. Treat them well, with respect, and always be a gentleman.

I hope life brings you years filled with adventure, wonder and love. While I want to shield you from sadness, grief and trauma, I know I can't; but I hope to arm you with enough resilience, strength and support to help you weather whatever adversity comes your way.

There are so many things I want you to learn, which I know I cannot teach you. Wisdom, courage, gratitude and a love and respect for nature, animals and humankind – all these need to be learnt from experience.

They say it will go by in a blink, and so far they've been right. You're already a little man and, while I adore watching you grow and learn, I also dread the day when you no longer want me to sing you to sleep.

Tonight, though, you do, so I'll sing.

I bristle when I hear people call you a 'miracle child'. Yes, you're my miracle, undoubtedly, but so is every mother's child. They are, we all are, born from light and stardust. I'd call that miraculous.

Love forever, Mum

NOËLLA COURSARIS MUSUNKA

MODEL and ACTIVIST / Mother to JAMES JR. and CARA

"Write your own history, don't allow others to do so for you, because no one understands your path better than you."
Noëlla was five years old, living in her homeland of the Democratic Republic of Congo (DRC), when her father passed away in his sleep next to her. Her mother – grief-stricken, penniless and uneducated – sent her to Europe to build a better life. Noëlla had a challenging childhood and was moved between relatives, first in Switzerland, then Belgium. Over the years, her only contact with her mother was through a few phone calls and a handful of letters.

But Noëlla did find refuge. As a student, she excelled and, after a year studying business management in Switzerland, she moved to London to learn English. There, she was scouted as a model and relished the idea that she could send money home to her mother. When she returned to the DRC at the age of 18, Noëlla was shocked to see the poverty there and vowed to work to make a difference.

In 2007, Noëlla founded Malaika, a non-profit organisation dedicated to improving the lives of Congolese girls and their communities through education and health programs. Her passion now is to 'model with meaning', using her profile to raise awareness for causes she feels strongly about as a mother, feminist and believer in the fundamental human rights of education, health and opportunity.

"When Congolese parents do have money, they educate the boys. But if you educate girls, there's less pregnancy, less HIV infection, less poverty," says Noëlla. "We need to elevate the education of women. It empowers them. It moves the country forward. It matters."

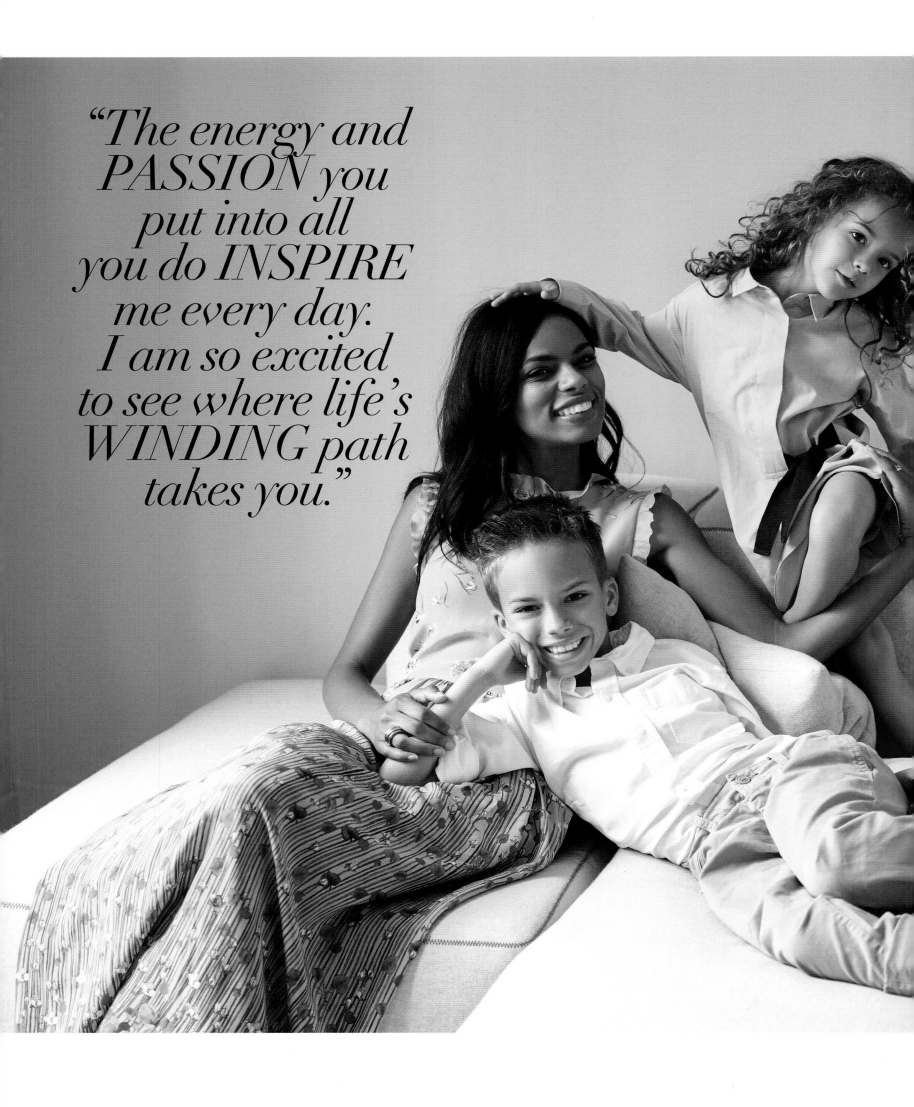

"The energy and PASSION you put into all you do INSPIRE me every day. I am so excited to see where life's WINDING path takes you."

Dear JJ and Cara,

You are the joys of my life. When I left the Democratic Republic of Congo so many years ago as a young girl, I could never have dreamed that I would one day return with my own children. My entire world had been turned upside down. I was only five years old and my father, your grandfather, had recently passed away. My mother made the most difficult decision of her life – a choice no mother should ever be faced with – to send me away to Belgium in the hope of providing me with a better life.

Life in Europe wasn't always easy and I missed my parents every day. But being away from home taught me the importance of bravery and perseverance and, above all, hard work – something I try to pass on to you both every day. The most precious gift I received in my new home was an education. It is this gift of knowledge, which would have eluded me in the Congo, that opened up a whole new world of possibility and promise. You are both growing up in very different circumstances from how I did, but I hope I have instilled these same values in you, and that they will serve you well as you embark on your own lives.

Remember to continue to always give back to those who have not had the same opportunities as you. For me, this meant giving back to the people of my first home, the country of Congo, and Africa overall. Opening a school for young girls in a village very close to where I was born, as well as building wells to serve the whole community, has been one of the most challenging and rewarding experiences of my life. It has been such a joy to get to share this with you both – watching you become incredible young philanthropists who have such a passion for caring for others.

I treasure the time I have spent with you in the Congo and at the school, teaching you about your ancestry and sharing my home country with you. It makes me so proud to see how proud you are of your heritage. And because of the school we built, hundreds of young women, many of them the same age as you both are now, are able to receive the priceless gift of an education, along with two healthy meals a day. Of course, it took a lot of special people to help me achieve this dream, and my advice to you is to surround yourself with people in your life who believe in your dreams, support you wholeheartedly and can help you fulfil your purpose.

Cara, my little girl, I love that you are so headstrong and determined. You are a natural-born leader destined to do incredible things, and I promise to always encourage this and support you in all that you do.

My darling JJ, you have such a kind heart and keen sense of fairness and diplomacy. I watch the way you not only take care of your little sister, but also your friends in the Congo. You are determined to help in any way you can – if they have no bed to sleep in or food to eat... or a football to play with!

Wherever you go and whatever you do, continue to carry the same joy for life that you have today. The energy and passion you both put into all you do inspire me every day. I am so excited to watch you grow up and see where life's winding path takes you. This is just the beginning.

I love you, Mummy x

PETA MURCHISON

CAMPAIGNER and FOUNDER of BOUNCE4BATTEN
Mother to MIA, TOBY and JASPER

We've had the privilege of profiling many inspiring women over the past five years on **The Grace Tales,** *but Peta Murchison's story is the most moving we've shared. In 2016, she bravely stood up and delivered a TedX talk at the Sydney Opera House, receiving a standing ovation and leaving the audience speechless. For nine years, she tirelessly cared for her daughter Mia, who was diagnosed with Batten disease, or late infantile neuronal ceroid lipofuscinosis (NCL) in 2013. This rare degenerative disorder affects about one in 100,000 children. By the time she was three, it had taken away Mia's ability to walk, talk and see. Last year, it took this beautiful angel's life at the age of nine.*

In 2014, Peta founded Bounce4Batten (celebrated annually on Batten Disease International Awareness Day on 31 March) inspired by Mia, who loved to bounce. The family hosted a party in their backyard with a jumping castle and trampoline, and invited friends to pop over for a bounce.
"The concept was for friends and family to promote awareness of Batten disease by bouncing and posting photos on social media. The joyfulness of bouncing delivered a message of awareness that resonated... One day soon we hope to play a part in finding a cure through supporting research via the national charity, Batten Disease Support & Research Association. Bounce4Batten is a simple concept, but we're hopeful it will make a positive splash and people will support a cause very close to our hearts."
Rest in peace Mia – you shone brighter in nine years than most people shine in a lifetime.

To my Darling,

I will remember you.

I will remember your long eyelashes – dark, full and so thick they criss-crossed each other with their slightly curled blonde tips. Your smudge nose, flushed cheeks and creamy, olive complexion. Your deep pink rosebud lips that would break into the widest of smiles, contagious and delightful.

I will remember your head tilted slightly back on the side, your soft, blonde curls falling down your shoulders, probably tangled underneath, and your wide, warm, happy, gappy, toothless face beaming at me.

I will remember burying my face and nuzzling your neck, and breathing in your sweetness – your lovely little sounds. Holding your body in my arms, positioning you so your head rested on my chest; tipping you forwards and bouncing you on my lap to see you smile, and that wild cackle laugh of yours.

I will remember the freckle on your right ear; the one on the side of your hand, just in-between your thumb and index finger; the one on your sternum; and the one in your belly button that I tried to wash away so many times, thinking it was dirt or chocolate.

I will remember the faint white scar in your hairline and the little white scar lines under your right nostril from the time you tumbled down the stairs and grazed your face as a two-year-old. Those two small, slightly raised round dots on your left thigh – the little bumps I felt as I ran my fingers across your thigh while you lay in my arms, tiny scars from your skin biopsy taken on the day we were given your diagnosis and the day our world shifted. The day I lay on the hospital bed with you as you peacefully slept. I will remember the sadness of this moment and the way your little body comforted me.

I will remember the shape of your hands and rounded ends of your fingers and toes – just the same as Joey's.

I will remember holding you on my chest for the first time, the most precious thing I'd ever held (until you came along, Toby, and you, Jasper).

I will remember you learning to crawl on a ferry trip heading to France. As soon as you could move, you wanted to be outside in the world. You would bang at the front door, demanding to get out, pushing your cart down the street or toy pram with Bunny and Dolly, regardless of how cold, wet or snowy it was outside in Dublin.

I will remember your little personality emerging, one of independence. A take-no-prisoners approach. A forceful, adventurous, entertaining and bossy toddler. You had your dad wrapped around your little finger and you would light up with joy when he arrived home or walked into a room.

I will remember the sweet abundance of love and jealousy you had for your new little brother, Toby; you smothering him with hugs and bossing him around. Toby adored you, his absolute favourite person.

I will remember your third Christmas and the excitement of opening your own roller bag. Of you hauling it behind you at high speed around our apartment in just your undies, followed in hot pursuit by your little brother, also wearing your undies.

I will remember things becoming more difficult for you as our confident daughter lost her balance. I will remember Toby catching up to you – and my pride in watching him accomplish things easily and the heartbreak of watching you struggle.

I will remember that you were always Miss Popular. You made special connections and friendships so easily. You were often the centre of affection. Poppy, Lukie and Evie adored you, often fighting over pushing your wheelchair or sitting next to you at horse riding.

I will remember pushing your pink, sparkly wheelchair down our street to school and across the playground, and without fail, someone would call out, "Hi, Mia!" They'd come and introduce themselves to me and tell me they were your friends – always so curious, gentle and honest.

I will remember that you, my darling, are the epitome of what is important: love, family, friendship, kindness and a meaningful life. Special people were drawn to you, and you to them. They held your hand, read you stories, propped your head up; adorned you with flowers, friendship bracelets, drawings, thousands of cards and handmade sensory books, trinkets. They danced with you and around you, requested to be in your group, put on performances for you, sat with you at playtime and loved you.

I will remember Hamish and I reminiscing about you. The dreams we had for you when you were born and the challenges we knew you'd give us in your teenage years. I will miss screaming at you to be kind to your little brothers, to clean up your room, to not stay out too late, to pay back that loan, to stay safe. I dreamed that you'd be a strong cyclist, enjoy the surf and find your own passions and love. Maybe horses would have been your thing. I dreamed that one day I might even hold your own child in my arms.

I wish I could have known this woman.

I will remember you lying with Jasper in your arms. I will remember him falling asleep with you tucked into the crook of your arm, and how relieved I felt that Jasper was sleeping peacefully, being kept nice and warm by you. And that you, my darling heart, felt the preciousness of a new baby.

I will remember relishing and marvelling at all Jasper's milestones, and that you, my darling, made every one of Jasper's smiles, peek-a-boo games and giggles that much sweeter.

I will remember how much Toby loved you and how proud he was to be your brother. I will remember his energy and love. That even when you were lying on your bed in the living area needing us to turn you and help you cough, you were surrounded by his enthusiasm. Listening to Toby charge around the house, playing music, dancing; and being yelled at to put his shoes on, have a bath, find his hat and brush his teeth. I will remember that Toby gave you his Doggie because we had lost Monkey.

I will remember all being together – Toby watching the *Peter Rabbit* movie in your room, quietly rearranging the flowers that surrounded you, and reading you a story.

I will remember that you brought us in tight as a family. We kept life as simple as we could and, through the swamps of sadness, we found our way, because you have always been my amulet and will be forever.

I will remember being with you during your last few weeks.

It was relentless.

I will remember leaning over you. Leaning in close, the top of our heads gently kissing. I whispered, "I'm so sorry, my darling, that you didn't get the life you deserved. We couldn't give you that. We all love you and you have given us so much."

Darling Mia, you are imprinted on our lives and in our hearts. You changed me, gave my life clarity and purpose. You shifted how I see the world reflected back at me. I will remember all the love and how, in our saddest moments, we felt so loved and how much everyone loved you.

Love, Mum

JORDAN REBELLO

MODEL / Mother to WYNTER POPPY

There's something about Jordan Rebello. With her beautiful curls, exotic brown eyes and cool vibe, she's the kind of mama that turns heads. Her father is from the Azores, off the coast of Portugal, and her mother is Native American. She grew up on Martha's Vineyard, in the USA. "It was such a beautiful childhood," she says. "It was a super-small town, so it had such a strong community. They say it takes a tribe to raise a child, and it's true."

Five years ago, Jordan became a mother to Wynter Poppy. Laid-back, honest and full of positive energy, she seems to have it all worked out. Her definition of success is simple: "It doesn't matter what you do for a living. It's about being happy," says Jordan. "Waking up and seeing the simple, beautiful things in life. If you can stay positive through it all – that's success to me."

Dear Wynter Poppy,

I was born and raised on a small island called Martha's Vineyard, on the coast of Cape Cod, surrounded by lots of family and a large community. You were also born there, in the same hospital as your mom and grandparents. I remember riding my bike all over town and running through the streets with my brothers. I have memories of building forts in the woods, riding on the back of the milk truck, exploring... Having a good childhood.
My parents were strict with certain things, like treating others with respect and having a good reputation in the community. But they were also relaxed when it came to most things, such as school grades and curfews. They let us be independent and make our own choices; to make mistakes and learn from them. I try to do the same – I encourage you to embrace your creativity, independence and individuality.
My role model is your grandmother, Mia. She's such a strong woman, who raised four children. I've always looked up to her and even more so now that I'm a mother. I always wanted to be a mom. I grew up being motherly to most of my friends. When I was pregnant, I felt that, even though I wasn't financially ready for a family (if there is such a thing), I had buckets of love to give to the child growing inside me. And that was *you*.
Children need guidance, support and discipline, but most importantly, they need love. Right now, you're in kindergarten. I still remember breastfeeding and cuddling you all the time. I find myself missing those moments, but then you'll tell me a funny joke and I remember that it is better to live in the now.
There is so much beauty shining through you. You go into most situations smiling. You're a good friend, you spread love, you're confident and you stand up for yourself. I want to be a mom who you can come to at any time. I want you always to find comfort in me. I want to be your home. I want to be someone you will look up to.
For me, achieving dreams is really about believing; staying positive when you fail; trying again and again. I've taught you to paint a picture of your dreams and then to set your mind on achieving them – I always find this makes your dreams more real. Don't let anyone tell you that you can't – always say, "I *can*."
A life lesson I am learning now, which I wish I had learnt when I was younger, is the way I react to aggravating situations. I find myself reacting instead of pausing. I want to teach you to pause and be idle at times of stress – to breathe and to be present. Because one day you'll be a grown-up, dealing with grown-up things. It all passes.
I love sharing all the firsts with you. I'm excited but full of nerves getting to watch you grow up. You have it all ahead of you – your first kiss, first dance, first job, first love, first break-up – and I'll always be there by your side.
Love, Mama

DAME HELENA MORRISSEY DBE

*FINANCIER and CAMPAIGNER / Mother to FITZROY, FLORENCE, TUPPY,
MILLIE, CLARA, OCTAVIA, THEODORE, CECILY and BEATRICE*

*"The first thing I do when I come in from work is to change into my 'home
clothes'," says Dame Helena. "On Friday evening, we relax over an early
supper together – sharing our news and how our day has gone – then watch
one of our favourite TV shows, all squashed together on a big sofa."*

It sounds like a perfectly normal way to unwind after a hard week, but for Dame
Helena, a hard week is developing a new ambitious personal investment business at
Legal and General, and there will be *nine* children sharing their news. Her stay-at-home
husband, Richard, whom she met at Cambridge, is a meditation teacher.
"To me, motherhood simply means love," she says. "Pure love. There is nothing
that compares to the outpouring of love – complete, pure and unconditional
– that I feel for my children."
In 2010, Helena established the 30% Club to campaign for greater female representation
on company boards. That goal achieved, she continues to campaign for gender equality.
In 2018, HarperCollins published her first book, *A Good Time to Be a Girl*. She is former
chair of the Eve Appeal, raising money for gynaecological cancers. In 2015, Helena
was recognised by *Fortune* magazine as one of the 'World's 50 Greatest Leaders', and,
in 2017, as the *Financial Times* 'Person of the Year' at its Boldness in Business Awards.

Dearest Fitz, Flo, Tuppy, Millie, Clara, Oki, Theo, Cecily and Bea,

Well, who could ever have imagined the joy? As I lay with tiny firstborn Fitz clutched to my chest – oblivious to the grim hospital and raging Hallowe'en storm outside, my afterbirth pains vanishing with love – I had a glimpse of what was to come. Nine of you, each beautiful and wondrous, yet so much greater together. Yesterday, you all sang *My Sweet Lord* at Florence and Benjamin's glorious wedding at home, looking and sounding so happy, bound by sisterly and brotherly love. It was a moment of indescribable joy.

Thank you. I am the happiest mother in the world.

As Dad and I have watched, listened, helped where we could, comforted where we could not, you have taught us so much over so many years, and there is, of course, more to come. Each of you has shown a strength, an inner compass that is unswerving and distinct, an ability to not let the fear of what might go wrong put you off from trying. When you falter, it is but briefly, and we marvel at that.

All of you have known disappointment and learnt that Winston Churchill was right to say that, "Success is not final, failure is not fatal: it is the courage to continue that counts."

As you become yet more independent, I pray that you keep hold of that resilience, that you lean on each other as well as us when you need to, that you help each other when your brother or sister needs you, and that you enjoy the strength of your unity.

We are already seeing the family dynamic change with Fitz, Flo and Tuppy's partners, and our beautiful first grandchild, Julian. It feels such a natural evolution, with the table that was laid for 11 now seating 15 and

> *"This is your life: feeling HAPPY and fulfilled is an ABSOLUTE, not a relative game. RECOGNISE when you feel most CONTENT and build on those MOMENTS."*

counting... I hope that, as your own lives unfold and you travel far, you keep coming back to us, knowing the unconditional love that awaits you.

Much of the advice I give to other young people comes from what you've taught me – and so I can only reinforce what you already know.

Leap before you look. Be open to possibilities, willing to explore and bold in your ambition. Push out your boundaries; you may well be surprised by just how much you can achieve.

Don't let the siren voices of convention limit you. Think big, start small, but start now. If you have an idea, don't worry about mapping out every step of the way. Focus on your vision and the path will open up.

Own the process. Play to your strengths – don't submerge the differences that define you. This is your life: feeling happy and fulfilled is an absolute, not a relative game. Recognise when you feel most content and build on those moments.

Remember there is no single 'right' path, no formula for success, no rule book about family or career. You may need to experiment before you find something or someone to love.

Find friends who genuinely want you to succeed. Look for a partner in life as well as in love. Keep away from those who belittle you. Never belittle others. Be kind, be generous. Help others where you can – it's very empowering, as well as a good thing to do.

Most importantly, remember you are, and always will be, very much loved.

Thank you again for being so wonderful.

With all my love, Mum xxx

INDIA HICKS

CO-FOUNDER of INDIAHICKS.COM
Mother to FELIX, AMORY, CONRAD, DOMINO and WESLEY

If there were a picture next to the definition of living life to its fullest,
it would be of model-turned-entrepreneur India Hicks. Born under a lucky
star (her grandfather was the last Viceroy of India, hence the name),
she was famously a bridesmaid to Princess Diana and is second cousin
to Prince Charles, who is also her godfather.

India's parents may be famed British interior designer David Hicks and Lady Pamela
Mountbatten, but she has never taken her life for granted; rather, filling it with
adventure. For some 20 years, India, her "other half", David Flint Wood, and their
family have lived on a remote island in the Bahamas only accessible by boat.
She is the co-founder and creative force of the lifestyle brand India Hicks
London-Harbour Island and a growing movement of entrepreneurial women.
Her five children grew up chasing snakes up coconut trees and playing pirates with
real machetes, surrounded by a menagerie of dogs, cats, love birds and a tortoise.
"Motherhood has taught me that I am last on the list," she says.
"And that's exactly how it should be."

"REMEMBER this – your childhood isn't who you are... It's just the OPENING chapter. You are the person who gets to WRITE the rest of the story."

To Felix, Wesley, Amory, Conrad and Domino,

As the tiny plane takes off over the turquoise waters and pink-sand beaches, and climbs higher and higher, further away from our home here in the Bahamas, I lean back and close my eyes. Finally, no phone ringing, no decisions to be made, no meeting scheduled, no dog needing to be walked. A moment alone to look down at the island disappearing out of sight and think just how extraordinary it has all been.

As I have told you often, nothing was really expected of me except to marry sensibly and live quietly in the English countryside. I went to a school where I was encouraged to sew and do needlepoint, and we had to wear a second pair of knickers over our knickers, just in case someone ever caught sight of the first pair of knickers, as that would have been shocking and unladylike.

My mother knew trouble was brewing when I opted to go to school in Scotland, where they could not care less if I even *wore* knickers, as long as I paid attention to the school motto: *Plus est en vous* ('There is more in you').

These words meant little to me while shivering in Scotland for a few years, then feeling lost afterwards, not entirely sure of myself. But from the moment I became a mother, I understood the galaxy of change that followed. This was the purpose of my life. You are the purpose in my life.

Raising a family on a small island in the middle of the Caribbean is not without its challenges. But your father and I had found each other here; he was shoeless and suntanned, running a small hotel with a copy of Joseph Conrad's *An Outcast of the Islands* in one hand and a Bloody Mary in the other. Four months later, I was pregnant with you, Felix, my beloved, stormy firstborn child.

We never married. We didn't feel the need. Somehow, being strangers in a strange land bound us more than any ceremony ever could. Hibiscus Hill, our home, provided us with the blank canvas upon which we could paint our own story, and what followed was not only an enduring relationship with one another, but also with island life.

Wesley, you appeared just a little after Felix. I have a picture beside my bed of you together, standing naked by the garden gate, aged about two years old – one black bottom and one white bottom, brothers for life. How thankful I am that you became my child.

When I think of our life, I imagine I am running on our beach at sunrise with the dogs. Most of you are still asleep in the house while I run. The small town across the dunes behind me stirs beneath a blanket of breaking dawn. I can hear the faint cry of cockerels strutting along the lanes; the smell of salt air and casuarina trees floats down to the water's edge. As I return, Conrad, you pass me on the path, sleepy but hopeful, surfboard in hand, in search of the perfect wave. Your enthusiasm is infectious.

The architecture and view from the harbour have hardly changed in the past 200 years, although many layers of time are faintly visible, just as they are in our own lives. It is unthinkable that family life will not change. It has been changing slowly from the beginning and will go on changing far into the future.

Amory, your wild and beautiful imagination has always been fuelled by island life. When asked by your father why you had attacked and shredded the banana tree he had been cultivating for so many months, you replied with such childish honesty: "I thought it was a ghost."

And Domino, you have grown up in the true spirit of the Bond girl you are named after. You cheer me on, encourage me, teach me, lift my heart and point me towards a horizon where women can stand stronger together, to live more extraordinary lives. We can only hope that, as we move forward, we remember and prize the simple memories this life together has offered us.

The greatest gift I have ever received is the love from you all, my five children. Remember this – your childhood isn't who you are. It's the beginning of who you are. It's just the opening chapter. You are the person who gets to write the rest of the story. So write a good one, never forgetting 'There is more in you'.

With love from your mother, India

CARLA OATES

FOUNDER of THE BEAUTY CHEF / Mother to JEET and OTIS

It was her experience as a child with eczema and allergies that would eventually inspire Bondi-based Carla Oates to create a career based entirely on 'beauty beginning in the belly' – or good gut health. When Carla was 13 years old, her mother – a former fashion editor – took her to see a naturopath, and it was there that she saw firsthand the connection between food and skin health.

Carla began her career as a fashion and beauty writer, and, after discovering how many synthetic substances there were in commercial beauty products, began making her own natural range of boosts and inner beauty powders from plants and organic foods. Her very first product, GLOW Inner Beauty Powder, made with 24 skin-loving bio-fermented and probiotic superfoods, has gained a cult following. On motherhood, she says, "I love Gilda Radner's quote: 'It is the glorious life force. It's huge and scary – it's an act of infinite optimism.'"

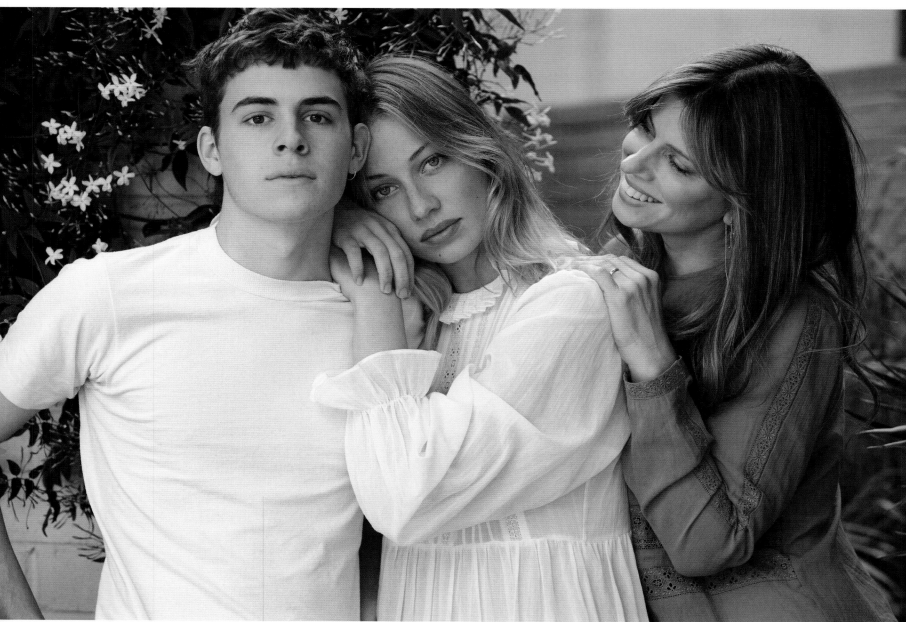

Dear Jeet and Otis,

You both woke me at midnight last night. Otis, you were out with your friends and texted me. "Mum, Jonathan Richman is just so cool," was your revelation, after we'd spent the afternoon together discussing great songwriters.

And then, Jeet... I started worrying about something you had confided in me and how you want to live in New York, which left me wide-eyed for hours. Maybe I could enrol you in design school or that pottery course in Brooklyn? Maybe we could all move there and Otis could go to music school...

Sitting here this morning, sleep-deprived as I was when you were babies (I was never good at control-crying – how could I ignore your desperate cries to be cuddled?), I feel a connection to you both that consumes me, fills me with joy and pulls at my heart all at once.

I love that you want to share with me what motivates and deflates you, inspires you and confounds you, and all the feelings and ideas we have discussed, pulled apart and resolved (or not) on our walks together. One hundred laps of Centennial Park later, we've witnessed the changing hues of leaves and little cygnets sitting confidently, but still unknowingly fragile, safe on their mums' backs.

The responsibility of motherhood, which I thought would ease as you grew up, has compounded. Somehow, life is more serious and I feel a strong need to hold you closer – to carry you on my back, warm, safe and secure.

Each day since I carried you protected in my belly, you've been a step closer to being your own people and less within my grasp. I'm becoming less responsible for the paths, people and places you choose to explore, and, while your growing independence truly scares me, it also intrigues and delights me. I believe in you both.

And, although it was I who gave birth to you, you both delivered a revised and better me. You switched on receptors that opened up new pathways in my brain and being, one of unconditional love – called motherhood – which is the best thing I've ever accomplished. It's also something I'm still trying to conquer, often stumbling, sometimes triumphing, at times overwhelmed, but always learning. For that I am truly grateful to you both.

Jeet, you've always been determined and strongly independent, and this has taught me about acceptance. With my plan to have a natural birth, it felt like you did everything in your power to challenge me, with a 36-hour labour requiring every drug and non-natural interventional tool to get you out, short of an emergency caesarean.

As a child, you refused to wear 'nice' natural clothing; instead preferring synthetic, 'cool teenage' clothing. And you would wince and say, "Why can't we have packet food?" I'm sure part of you was laughing at my 'kale and paisley cotton dress' sensibility, with your beautiful, intelligent, wry sense of humour. I am constantly in awe of your unique world view, your acute eye for beauty, design and the ridiculous. What an amazing artist of life you are.

Otis, your persistence, passion and romantic idealism are wonderful. The patience you taught me as you emerged from the womb. Not walking, you galloped and whinnied with your absolute love of horses, your childhood spent pretending to be either the horse or the cowboy – *The Man From Snowy River*. The years and years (and years) of your desperate pleas for a horse. That passion is now channelled into your music and art, and your talent for composing songs that people love because it's a reflection of your beauty, sensitivity and depth. You are truly golden.

When you were both little, you'd ask me why we weren't rich. Jeet, you'd say, "My friend Molly, she lives in a kingdom!" You'd both roll your eyes and sigh when I responded with, "Yes, but we are so very rich in love!"

We had the best teacher when it came to acceptance and unconditional love. How lucky were we to have your Nan? My beautiful, kind, ever-graceful mum taught us about love without judgement, resentment, malice or conditions. She loved you almost as much as I do. I didn't think I could love anyone as much as my mum until I had you. It was this reservoir of love and strength that nurtured us through her protracted illness and passing. You were always by her side and mine, wholly and unwaveringly, making my heartache and pain bearable. Thank you. I am so proud of you both.

She lives through us in our smiles, the way we love, and our love of food. She is omnipresent in Mother Nature – in the nurture and embrace of a canopy of trees, the soothing sound of the waves (as she'd say in times of stress, "Let the waves wash over you"), the joy of sunflowers and her love of magpies – her loyal friends.

I don't know where the time has gone. As we walk around Centennial Park, the cygnets are now beautiful swans, but as they swan about in their 'independence', their mums still keep a watchful eye.

The world is ripe for the picking as you leave your nest, smart, creative, sensitive, strong, caring and capable, ready to embrace and navigate all its wonders. My wish is that you look for the beauty in everything and stay connected to who you are, your roots, dreams and desires. Keep your smarts about you and follow your gut – if something or someone doesn't feel right, it probably isn't. See mistakes as growing pains. Don't let them define you, and know I am always here to guide you, love you and catch you if you fall.

I'll finish with a quote from a book I would read to you when you were little, *Oh The Places you'll Go!* by Dr Seuss.

Out there things can happen, and frequently do, to people as brainy and footsy as you. And when things start to happen, don't worry, don't stew. Just go right along, you'll start happening too! Just never forget to be dexterous and deft. And never mix up your right foot with your left. You're off to great places, today is your day, your mountain is waiting – so get on your way.

Love, your Mum xx

ELLE STRAUSS

FASHION DIRECTOR and STYLIST / Mother to HONOR and IMOGEN

Elle Strauss's eye for style was honed in London, where she worked as a stylist at Elle, GQ, *and* Company *magazines. She met her husband, photographer James Dimmock, on a shoot for* The Face *(where she began her career as fashion assistant), when he caught her burning a shirt with the iron. They moved to New York, where she became senior fashion editor for the Condé Nast magazine* Lucky. *A fashion directorship at online retailer Shopbop followed, before she returned to Condé Nast as fashion director of* Brides.

Growing up in Leigh-on-Sea in Essex, England, Elle recalls, "My mum was a dancer, and always incredibly stylish in an understated way, I like to think I got my love for fashion from her and my grandma – she could open a shop with her shoe collection."
Elle takes the same down-to-earth approach to motherhood as she does to fashion.
"I think at times it all just feels rather overwhelming," she says. "Trying to juggle everything and then getting out of the house, and making the lunches and making sure everyone's washed and dressed. And then your seven-year-old suddenly decides she doesn't like her shoes… You feel like your head's going to explode. During those moments, I literally just sit down, take a deep breath and tell myself it's ok to be late, because it really isn't a big deal. No one's going to die, and the worst thing that's going to happen is that you'll be late!"

*"Watching you
LEARN and grow
into the beautiful,
KIND and
SMART human
beings you
have become is
MAGICAL and
humbling."*

Dear Honor and Imogen,

I want to start this letter by saying that I love you both very much and I'm so proud of you. Both of you make your dad and me laugh and cry with joy (and frustration at times!), and wish that you would stay our little girls forever and never grow up. Despite your five-and-a-half-year age gap, you guys are the best of friends and play so well together – it's brilliant! Even last night in the bath, after crazy splashing and half the bath water ending up on the floor, you were cracking each other up playing mermaids and laughing at me when I told you off for all the water!

You guys are wonderful and a pain in the butt, all at the same time. There was no roadmap for raising you, but we are doing the best we can. Watching you learn and grow into the beautiful, kind and smart human beings you have become is magical and humbling. You have transformed my life forever. I never knew that I was capable of such love.

Honor, your kindness in life and patience with your lil' sis makes my heart burst. When your teacher described you as her "angel", it left me in tears. We are so proud of how you transitioned to Los Angeles from New York, and the positivity you've shown while joining a new school. I can't believe you are eight years old and about to start third grade. Eek! It feels like just yesterday that I took you home from the hospital in a yellow cab.

Imogen, your determination and humour constantly floor us. Despite you only being two and a half, your personality shines through bright and bold – from 'cooking us pasta', to your huge grins and the shaking of your gorgeous little bum. We waited a long time for you and you were worth the wait. Squidgy Woo, we love you.

Being your mummy has made me strong and vulnerable at the same time. I wish I could wrap you guys up and never let you go. But go and grow you must, and I will be with you every step of the way. I'm so lucky to be your mum and to be entrusted with your lives.

I love you both forever, your Mummy

JESSICA DINER

BEAUTY and LIFESTYLE DIRECTOR at BRITISH VOGUE
Mother to NOAH

With her refreshingly relatable take on parenthood, far removed from the stereotypes surrounding one of the world's most glamorous magazines, Jessica Diner balances the delicate seesaw of children and a career with charm, humour and grace.

Having joined British *Vogue* at the age of 22, and worked her way up to the position of beauty editor, Jessica moved to online beauty site Birchbox as content and creative director in 2014. She returned recently to *Vogue* as its beauty and lifestyle director. Concerned that becoming a mother might hold her back, the truth is that it has done anything but. Now, she manoeuvres between her "dream job" and her adorable three-year-old son, Noah, juggling it all, if not with ease, then with good humour. The only thing she admits has gone by the wayside is her social life. "It's less about balance, more about being an expert juggler and prioritising your time," says Jessica. "To be blunt – it's about getting shit done."

My Noah,

As I write this, you're sleeping in the room next door. If I love you all-consumingly when you're awake, my heart swells to the point of brimming over at the thought of you asleep. Sleeping so peacefully and so contentedly in your cot.

More than just being a time for respite and recuperation, to me, your deep sleep is a subconscious representation of your happiness and fulfilment. I've always taken it as a sign that you feel safe – safe enough to allow yourself to drift off into a dream. This week, you told me you had "a marvellous dream". You didn't disclose the details, but it really made me laugh. I often wonder what you dream about and where you are when you're in your dream world. What do you see? What do you do? Who else is there with you? Is it just an extension of your waking hours, limitless in their imagination?

I love how you sleep, because for so long you didn't. Those first 10 months felt like snatched fragments of time: you and I tussling to 'nap well', 'sleep through' or 'have a routine'... All those expected milestones that mothers like to throw around competitively as badges of honour didn't really happen for us. The majority of the first year, if we're to be totally honest, my darling, was tough for us both – you in a constant state of reflux.

But here we are, you and I, joined at both the hip and the heart, completely inseparable, completely one. I often look at you and can't actually believe that I made you and that you are mine. I could look at you for hours – examining every eyelash, fingernail or tooth, your soft, radiant and luminous skin – processing how it's all come from the crazy culmination of your father and me.

People tell me constantly how much you look like your father. You're his carbon copy, they might say. That you're nothing like me is often what follows. I protest, I jest, I laugh. But it doesn't really matter, because, while you may not look like me, you *are* me. And it's you and me against the world.

To see that world through your eyes is one of the most humbling experiences I've ever had. To see someone do something for the first time – it's pretty bloody amazing – swimming, going on a bus, going to the zoo, blowing bubbles, making music... Simple, everyday things viewed and received with wonderment. It's truly grounding.

As we continue through our many firsts together, it's a constant reminder to appreciate the little things, but also to never sweat the small stuff. I like to think that I'm guiding you and helping you navigate your way through these formative years, but the reality is that every day you're leading the way.

What power you possess in your little soul. You've taught (and continue to teach) me patience, resilience, love, kindness, compassion, determination... I've learnt more about myself in the past few years than I've learnt in my lifetime. Long may this continue.

Because, while being a mother isn't always easy, being *your* mother has exceeded all expectations. Motherhood, to me, is about looking past all the logistics, expectations and practicalities to see you as a person and to support you into being the best version of yourself you can be at every age. The responsibility that comes with this role is hands down the hardest, but most rewarding thing I have ever done.

In setting out to write this letter (which, by the way, was much harder than I thought it would be – there's so much to say and yet there aren't enough words), I thought it would be me pinning down my hopes and dreams for you. But I soon realised that they aren't for me to set out, they are for you to create, using the unique magic that is instilled within you.

Instead, this letter has become a letter of thanks. A love letter of sorts, to say thank you for being you and for opening up my eyes to the world and its wonder.

So every night when you go to sleep and we say, "Love you boo," as is our little ritual, while I'm not sure if you know what the word 'love' actually means yet, I know that you feel it, and I hope that it stays with you into your "marvellous dreams".

May you sleep well tonight and every night, and may your tomorrows continue to be days filled with love, excitement and discovery.

Thank you for being you, and thank you for being the making of me.

Love you boo xx

COLLETTE DINNIGAN

FASHION and INTERIOR DESIGNER
Mother to ESTELLA and HUNTER

*The first designer to take Antipodean style to the catwalks of Paris,
Collette Dinnigan became a Fashion Week stalwart, showing there
for nearly two decades. But for South African-born Collette, no career
success or honour can compare to her role as a mother.*

"I believe children need routines, consistency and assurance," she says. "These
things don't come from a textbook; they come from your gut, your heart and
instinct. I need to be around much more to teach them these things."
So, in 2013, she closed her boutiques in Sydney, Melbourne and London, and is
now finding the balance between collaborations and design projects, and precious
time with her family. In 2017, she was awarded Officer of the Order of Australia.

Dear Hunter and Estella,

As I write this, Hunter, you are almost six years old. I was 48 when you arrived and it was a magical time for all of us, especially for you, Estella, because all you had wished for was a baby brother and finally you got one. You were eight years old at the time. That was one of my most vivid memories of motherhood. And then of course, the year we spent in Italy together as a family. We had a base in Rome and travelled around the country – Sicily, the Amalfi Coast, Puglia... What we realised was, the smaller the place, the better it was for all of us. You'd share a bed and it was a fantastic bonding time for you both. I often think that, had we not done that trip, you might not be as close as you are now, because of your age difference.

I hope you never forget our time in Positano, where we spent our days jumping on and off the boat, and eating pizza and pasta – all the things you love doing. And the school you went to in Rome. Hunter, you loved going on the big bus with your sister.

We went to Italy partly because I wanted to get out of the spotlight in Australia, but also because I wanted to spend time with my family. That was the entire premise for changing my business.

You both have great attention to detail; you don't miss a trick. You're very worldly and I think that's as a result of travelling a lot with me. You're both emotional, very kind and gentle, and you love animals; but you're also quite feisty and don't hold back your opinions.

I've wanted always to give you a safe place; that was always a priority. But I also wanted to give you a sense of freedom. I've tried to create a world that's real and isn't a cocoon, to give you a bigger space to explore. It's why we moved from the city to the country.

The motto I live by now is: 'Be present in the moment, and don't try to do five things at once'. If you are both home after school, I won't be on the phone. I try to do one thing and do it properly, rather than multitask. Before I had children, all I did was multitask.

I see so many other mothers who are so present in every moment of their children's lives. I often wish I could be that mother, but I'm not. I try hard, but in other ways: I have the courage to make the decision to move countries or to do a road trip, to do things out of our comfort zone, and I think this has shaped you both in different ways.

I've had the confidence to do these things because of the experience of running my own business. I hope I can pass on my confidence to you both. Always trust your instincts in making decisions and remember, if you fail, it's not a problem.

Estella, you're totally disinterested in dresses – you're a horse-riding girl who lives in jeans and tops. Hunter, you make me laugh when you say, "Oh Mummy, you're quite famous, you know, in the newspapers and magazines, and everyone says you make the best dresses. I'm so proud of you." You're also a boy's boy – you especially love soccer.

I've taught you good manners, kindness and how to look after people less fortunate, as well as each other. I've taught you how to appreciate what's right in front of you.

Right now, when I ask you what you want to do when you grow up, you both tell me you want to work with animals. Whatever you do, just work really hard and something will happen; people will notice. But don't do it to be noticed; do it because you're passionate about it.

That's what I did. I chose something I was passionate about. I didn't necessarily think I wanted to be in Paris or London; I was driven to do something unique. I approached my career wanting to do things differently and doing things first. So follow your heart, trust your instincts, be honest and work hard. Nothing will ever beat that. And if you don't do well, try something else. Don't be afraid.

I was born in Africa, educated in New Zealand and started my business in Australia, and there were moments when it was lonely. I had no family or school-friend connections. Everything I did was always for the first time. In the past couple of years, I've transitioned my career in a whole different direction. I do a lot of interiors, which I love, and still work very much with textiles and colour, so I'm very fortunate.

I worked very hard at a high level through my 20s and 30s, but there was a price for that, too. I was working seven days a week, missing out on a lot of other opportunities that younger people have. But now I'm reaping the benefits. I have a new-found confidence, in that I feel it's not always about the money; it's about the lifestyle, about the decisions you make. Big isn't necessarily better. Life is about what makes you happy and what makes you laugh, and everyone has different needs. It's about finding balance and this can take time. Life is also about having courage – to make decisions such as moving to another country.

We're going to live between Italy and Australia, and you will both grow up speaking two languages and experiencing both lifestyles, which I think will be invaluable.

I've taught you to have your own voice and not to condemn others; to be kind and humble, well mannered and non-judgemental. Always focus on how you are as a person. When you look back, you won't feel good if you were awful to others. If you're a trusting, loving, kind person, you will always walk away knowing you did the best you possibly can.

Love, Mummy xxx

DANA STEPHENSEN

SOLOIST at THE AUSTRALIAN BALLET and
HOLISTIC HEALTH COACH / Mother to JASPER

Dana Stephensen began dance training in her hometown of Brisbane when she was three years old, moving to Melbourne to attend The Australian Ballet School at the age of 16. But at barely 20 years old, she was diagnosed with Hashimoto's thyroiditis. "The importance of health and wellbeing is integral to being able to dance professionally," explains Dana, "but my body – the very thing that allowed me to dance – was slowly breaking down, and I was not in control."

On her journey to recovery, Dana trained as a certified holistic health coach. She is currently studying to be a nutritionist as she learns to live with the daily ups and downs of thyroid disease while managing a high-functioning career and demanding performance schedule. "It's a daily juggle to find the balance," she says, "and I would like to inspire others to listen to their bodies... source the help they need, get well and be able to achieve their dreams."
Since joining the company full-time in 2005, she has won the Telstra Ballet Dancer Award and, in 2014, became a soloist, dancing the roles of Giselle, and Dawn in *Coppelia*, among many others. But for Dana, no role is more important than that of mother to her beloved son, Jasper.

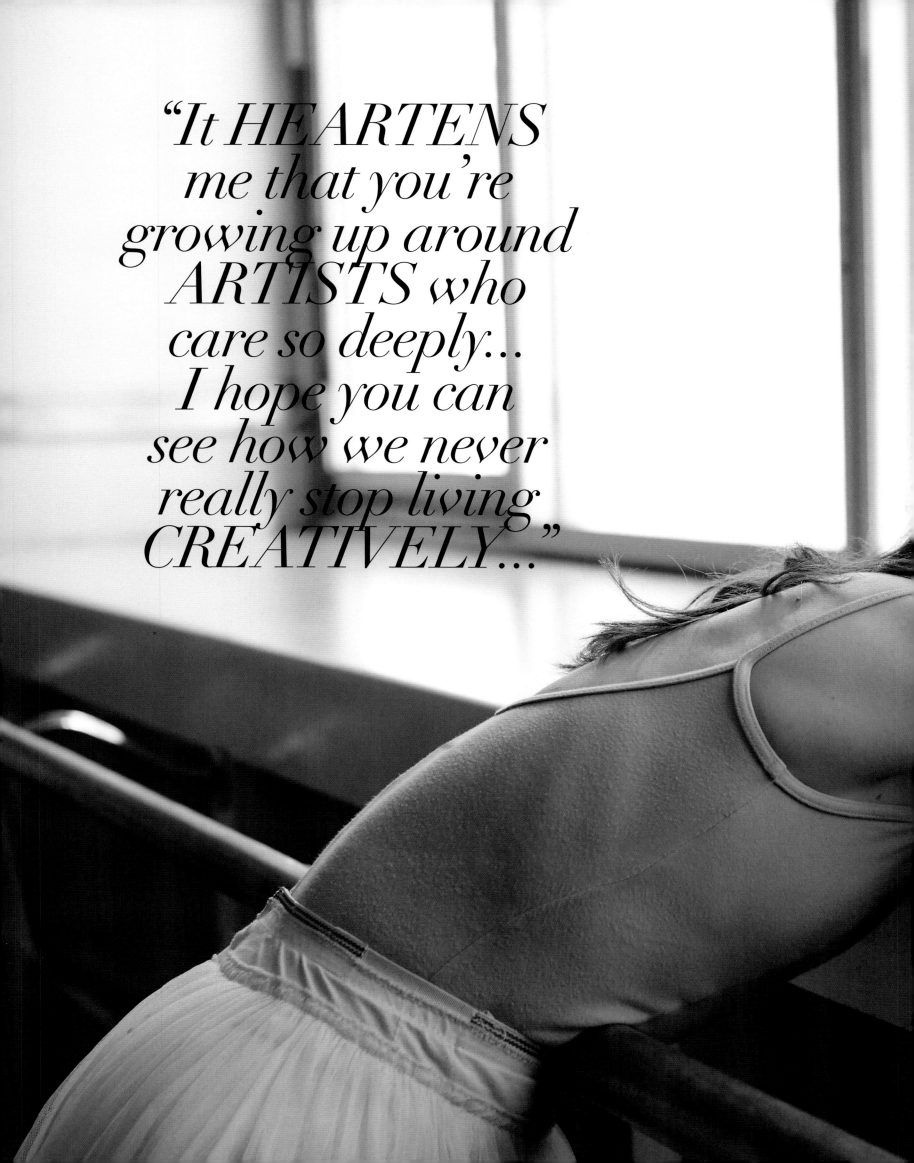

"*It HEARTENS me that you're growing up around ARTISTS who care so deeply… I hope you can see how we never really stop living CREATIVELY…*"

Dearest Jasper,

When I see you running with such abandon, I see your whole body charged with energy, your face euphoric, your eyes ablaze with life itself. You are completely enthralled by sensation, your spirit is soaring.

And I smile because we are so similar, my darling. This is me on the stage – it's my happy place.

When you were nine months old, I returned to the stage dancing the iconic ballerina role of Giselle. I have many precious dancing memories, but this performance was something so rare, so exquisite. I stepped into the lights that day a new mum, a different woman, an artist transformed. I danced with a freedom, a tenderness and an unparalleled sense of love in my heart.

It was all because of you – my love for you. You were waiting backstage for me and I wrapped you in my arms. I was living my dreams.

That day set the scene for a second lease of life for my career, an even more passionate one. You take it all in your stride. Your eyes light up watching the dancers, and the Sydney Opera House is your all-time favourite playground. I know it can be difficult for us, sometimes, with Mummy working long hours and travelling around the country. I worry that I'm not enough for you. I feel guilty and selfish for being so driven to follow my own dreams when I should be helping you chase yours. But you also deserve a Mummy who is learning how to be a better human each day in the best way she knows. We both have the brightest twinkles in our eyes this way.

It heartens me that you are growing up around artists who care so deeply, who drive themselves every day to move people. People who wear determination and sacrifice like sweat on their skin, who push beyond limitations each day to create magic. I hope you can see how we never really stop living creatively, that creativity runs through our veins long past childhood.

We often speak about our "big feelings" and how it feels like we should put a lid on them, especially those ugly 'sad' or 'angry' ones. They all count, sweetie. They are just as real and should be honoured just the same. They whisper important things to us, too. I hope you grow up knowing that it's ok to hurt, to have cared so much your heart is aching, to feel lost at times.

The only way I can teach you about people is to show you that I'm a perfectly imperfect one: one who makes mistakes, who loves and grieves equally. Someone who finds the world both a delight and a sensitive place. I hope that, by showing you my vulnerabilities, you can make friends with yours.

Our similarities make me smile – the unbridled excitement and recklessness, but also the tenderness that people least suspect in bright sparks like us.

It's this sensitivity speaking when you cup my face in your little hands and say, "Mummy, you're ok. You're my best friend." At three, you already care so much for people, it just astounds me.

It can be hard in life, and the ballet world especially, when so much seems subject to personal opinion. I've learnt it's best not to let the passing thoughts of others take up permanent residence in my heart. Sift for the gold and gracefully leave the rest.

Turning up and putting yourself in the arena counts for more than you know. Hard work brings the good luck. Be open to giving something a go and being courageous, especially when you feel like you can't. I promise something good will come of it.

Your ideas on what you want in life will change over time, and that can be liberating but also a bit scary. Over the years, I hope you grow to trust your sense of intuition. Be open to people changing your life: some people are the most beautiful surprises. When you feel your heart exploding in your chest, trust that it means something magnificent. Love is magnificent. Let in the magic.

Always remember the unique spark you bring to the world. I saw it the second you were born. No matter how stormy the days, that light never goes out. I hope you always feel brave enough to show how much you care and you're never too proud to smile, to cry or to say, "I'm sorry." I hope you laugh as freely as you do now through all of your days.

I wish you many moments that take your breath away. Like tonight, staring in wonder at the full moon together. I said to you, "Darling, isn't it spectacular?"

You asked me what spectacular meant. I said, "It means all kinds of wonderful." You beamed at me and said, "Mummy... I love wonderful."

You are a wonder.

Love, Mummy xx

> *"I hope you grow up knowing IT'S OK to hurt, to have CARED so much your heart is aching, to FEEL lost at times."*

FIONA JOLLY

CHILDREN'S FURNITURE DESIGNER / Mother to POPPY and HARRYO

As her name suggests, Fiona Jolly's boundless enthusiasm has never allowed her to stay still for long. She was just 17 when, following her dreams, she went to London to make it in the beauty world, and soon was jetting all over the globe, working with everyone from Kylie Minogue to Goldie Hawn. But she found herself in a very different situation when her girls arrived. Suddenly, the life of an international makeup artist was impossible with two small children, so Fiona decided to put down her brushes for the final time.

"I used to feel lost when people asked what I did," she says. "For 24 years, makeup had been my life. I did start writing about beauty for magazines from home, but it wasn't the same." Instead, she turned her attention to country life with her husband and menagerie of dogs, cats and ponies. But it wasn't long before the old enthusiasm took hold again and Fiona was onto her next project – setting up her furniture business for children, Reasons to be Jolly, from an outhouse on her property. And in true Jolly style, she's never been happier.

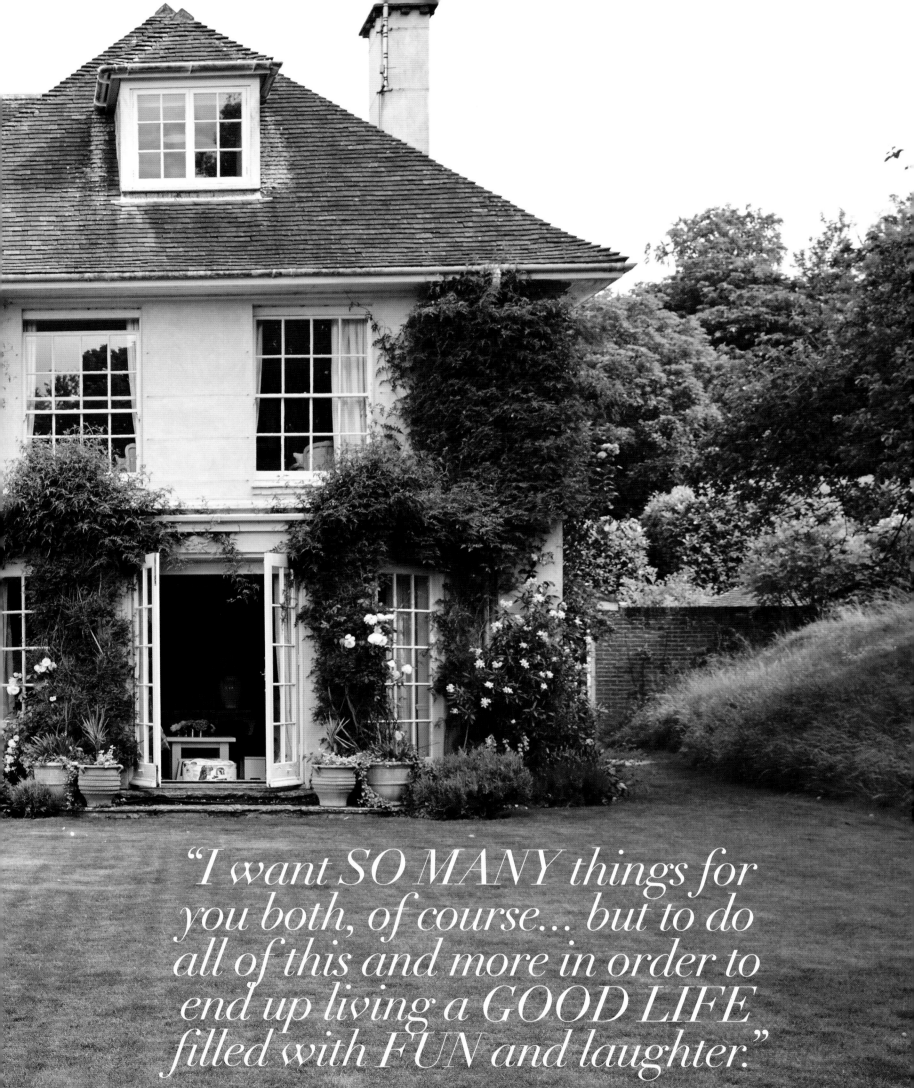

"I want SO MANY things for you both, of course... but to do all of this and more in order to end up living a GOOD LIFE filled with FUN and laughter."

Darling Poppy and Harryo,

It is hard to believe sometimes when I look at you, that for most of my life, you didn't exist. You two gorgeously complicated individuals weren't even alive yet. More extraordinary still is when I listen to you talking to me as if my only reason for existence *is* you. At the airport yesterday, we stood together, waiting for Daddy to organise the rental car. Poppy, you looked at me with your big, beautiful eyes and exclaimed, "Mummy, you are so lucky you have Daddy. If you didn't, you wouldn't be able to travel."

So, I explained to you and Harryo about how I had travelled the world on my own, from the age of 18, with my super-heavy black box of makeup, painting the faces of some of the world's most glamorous women and men. I told you all about the things you can do on your own as a woman. Girls can be anything they want to be – strong, independent and, most important, free. I look forward to you both going out there into the world and seeing the wonders it holds for you, as women.

Sometimes, I find it helps me having a little motto running through my head. My favourite is 'No guts, no glory'. For me, life's all about being brave and active with your mind and body, not comparing yourself to others, and allowing yourself to follow your dreams. Which leads me nicely to the other motto often on loop in my head: 'Compare and despair'. Don't waste your time looking left and right at what other people are doing. Just keep focused on the future, and your ideas and visions for it. Don't follow the masses and be ordinary; be brave and be extraordinary.

Of all the things I would wish you to have, and, in my opinion the key to a happy life, is a good sense of humour! The ability to laugh at life even when it's serving you lemons. The skill in finding the funny even when it may be a hard situation. Of course, there are moments of sadness and loss, but the art of not sitting and wallowing is a fantastic one to learn – the skill of knowing when you are down, then picking yourself up, shaking yourself off and finding the lighter side of the situation. Don't worry, don't stress; just trust and move forward with enthusiasm and a smile.

Gravitate towards like-minded people, for life will be a lot more fun with them beside you. Surround yourself with them – work with them, eat with them and, later on, date them and marry them. Because with those people in your life, it will be more fun and more positive. They will help make sense of the world. Whatever the problems, together, you will find that thin thread of humour and follow it until it becomes a belly laugh.

I have always loved having the name Jolly. It made me work towards living up to it! Expectations were set. No one expects a miserable Jolly, but I'm afraid that's exactly what I was when I was your age. I went through school with a frown, feeling like someone owed me happiness. But once I left school, I made a conscious decision to change one thing – I decided to smile, even when I didn't feel like it. Before I knew it, I was always smiling without trying. I lightened up and started enjoying myself; stopped beating myself up about not being perfect. I stopped comparing myself and my life with others.

From that point on, life got happier. I met great friends who I've stayed close to my whole life, through good and bad. It helped me break down walls with people and break into the makeup world, even on my travels with people who didn't speak the same language. I worked in a freelance market and would often get jobs because people liked the idea of a 'Jolly' makeup artist.

When I married Daddy (Jamie, to me), I gave up that name, which I found hard. But I knew change was good and I was heading to the most important role of my life, motherhood. I put Jolly among your middle names, just sneaked it in there as third on the list. I remember people saying, "Two girls – I'm sure they will be pretty." I would think, *pretty*? I want them to have a good sense of humour.

When you were little and wanted a treat, I would say, "Sure, if you can make me laugh." Your little faces would screw up deep in thought and then you would surprise me with a joke or song: "What did the 0 say to the 8? Nice belt." But as the years go on and I watch you enjoying a good joke or watching a funny movie and holding your sides with laughter, and how you can repeat the joke back weeks later and laugh like it's the first time you've heard it, I couldn't be happier or more proud.

It's hard sometimes for you both, with a father who writes comedy and a mother who's pushing a little to lighten you up. I know it sometimes feels like teasing, but I want to try and lighten the situation. I know you may have just fallen off your chair that only had three legs, but you did look very funny the moment you remembered, too late, that it was the chair *not* to sit on.

I want so many things for you both, of course: to be successful in everything you want to do; to find your own interests, be enthusiastic and work hard. But to do all of this and more in order to end up living a good life filled with fun and laughter.

There's a picture outside your bedroom door of a dog wearing shades, sitting in a tiny boat, with his paws behind his head and a smile on his face. He's bobbing along in what looks like the middle of an ocean. Under the picture in huge type are the words: 'He knows not where he's going, for the ocean will decide – it's not the destination... but the glory of the ride.' The dog's got it right.

Love, Mummy xxxx

KATE RITCHIE

ACTOR, AUTHOR and *RADIO PRESENTER / Mother to MAE*

"Tired, generous and (quietly) ferocious" is how one of Australia's most beloved media personalities, Kate Ritchie, describes herself. In person, she's strikingly beautiful, down-to-earth, intelligent and instantly likeable. The actor, author, radio presenter and mother has been in the spotlight since she was a child, having spent more than 20 years playing the character of Sally Fletcher on Home and Away. *With two Gold Logie awards under her belt, Kate has since moved onto radio, where she is one of the witty hosts on Nova's Drive show, with Tim Blackwell and Marty Sheargold.*

Kate's daughter, Mae, arrived in August 2014. "It was only this week I found myself trawling through photos of the moment I first met Mae and attempting to describe it to my expecting sister. No words will ever translate what my entire being felt at that time," she says. "What I do know is that, despite a small sense of relief that the job was done, unfortunately or fortunately, I will never feel anything quite like it in my life again. It was awesome, in the true sense of the word."
During her pregnancy, Kate was inspired to write her first children's book, *I Just Couldn't Wait To Meet You*, which captures the joy and anticipation of expecting a child. She has since written a second book, *It's Not Scribble to Me*, which was once again inspired by and penned for her little muse, Mae.

Dearest Mae,

Of all of the Mummas in all the world, thank you for choosing me to be yours, dear girl. When you were purely an angel baby and I was merely a woman with fleeting thoughts of who you might be, thank you for looking down and deciding on me; deciding I would be yours and you would be mine until the end of our earthly days.

Perhaps this is not really how mothers and their babies are brought together, but I kind of like to think so. There's something lovely about thinking that you spied me and thought we'd make a good team. So that on all those days when we are winning and, yes, even on the horrid ones, we can look at each other with love and know we are exactly where we're meant to be, on that team you chose many moons ago.

To be very clear, I would pick you right back a million times over. I promise I would. Because a life without you now seems unimaginable, somewhat pointless, even. Goodness knows who I'd be today if you hadn't come along to change everything. To change me, change my life and change my outlook – every inch of how I see this crazy world we are navigating our way through.

You see, Mummy existed long before you came along. It's hard to believe, I know. She was a little girl just like you and loved to dance just the same. She lived with Nanny and Pa, your aunties and uncle, and managed to survive her formative years. She loved and lost and learnt many things along the way. She was a young woman with many friends and a job that led people to believe they knew her. She brought happiness to many and hurt some feelings.

She made lots of the same mistakes multiple times and she made some good choices, too. She met your handsome and very cheeky Daddy, and then there was you – a tiny little person who I thought I would be in complete charge of. Ha!

A person whom I would nurture and teach and watch grow. Fingers crossed, I am consistently ticking these boxes for you, Bubba. But, my goodness, I have to say that most days, I feel you have taught me far more than I've ever taught you and I am so incredibly thankful.

You are so full of wonder, my precious Mae, and really are the only person in my world who allows me to simply be me. It will be a long time before you fully comprehend the enormity of this for your Mumma, but your arrival and the last four years we've spent together – showing each other who we are without any preconceived ideas or assumptions – is like nothing I have ever had the pleasure of experiencing before.

To you, I am your Mumma, that's all, and really, that's all I yearn to be. You see me exactly as I am; not what I've done before, who I've been before or what you've read. I am the very best version of me (the one I like most) when I'm with you, and cannot articulate the feeling of love and security that has given me – a calm freedom like never before.

I often wish you had existed in some form long ago, when I was being taught to be humble because of this silly job I have. Now I realise you can be humble and ferocious and ask for respect all at the same time. Humble does not mean weak. Humility can be executed with authority as well as grace. Always remember this. It's ok, I intend to remind you if ever you forget.

You've taught me patience, Mae. I'll admit I fail to exercise it every day, but I know it's there and thanks to you. You've taught me to pat myself on the back a little more; to care for less fortunate families, because I now know the value of support; to appreciate the value of equality; to make plans and use every day that we are lucky to be given; to realise I'm brave enough to have a go at anything.

One day, I will be instructing you to do the same, so I intend to lead by example. You are teaching me to accept myself and value myself, especially when it comes to my body. I never quite loved or appreciated it in the way I do now. If I can bring you into the world with all its might and power, then I suggest it deserves a lot more credit than it has been receiving all these years.

You've also taught me to stand up for myself and for girls. You're teaching me to love unconditionally and expect the same. To curb my foul mouth. To rejoice in the simple things.

My word, the list is long and our journey together is still young. I have faith there are some things I have taught you along our way, too. Things you will thank me for. Or not... I am positive they will show themselves, maybe not even until you are a woman yourself, knowing what I know now, and that is perfectly fine by me.

Until then, Mae, I am happy for you to hold my hand, exude joy, show the kindness that you do, and fill my heart with the knowledge that that is a part of me, the part of me I am most proud of.

I love you, Mae Katherine Ritchie Webb. You are my greatest gift, achievement and inspiration, and I will feel this way even when you're a teen slamming doors up the hallway in the same fashion I did. How awesome is that? To realise we have only just begun, dear girl.

Your Mumma xxx

> *"Goodness knows WHO I'd be if you hadn't COME along to CHANGE everything."*

WHITNEY BROMBERG HAWKINGS

ENTREPRENEUR / Mother to BARRON, SNOWDON and WALLIS

For the co-founder and CEO of London-based luxury flower delivery service Flowerbx, being immaculately presented has always helped her to aim high. Working as Tom Ford's right-hand woman for almost two decades, Whitney Bromberg Hawkings mastered the art of never letting standards slip, even while juggling the demands of three young children.

After growing up in Dallas, Texas, Whitney moved to New York to study French literature at Columbia University before heading to Paris. There, she landed a job as Tom Ford's assistant at Gucci. Over the course of her tenure, she became senior vice president of communications, as well as launching her own company in 2015. However, it wasn't until she was pregnant with her daughter, Wallis, that Whitney realised her business was more than a sideline. Now, her world is filled with flowers.

My darlings Barron, Snowdon and Wallis,

It goes without saying that you (and Daddy) are the best things that ever happened to me. You are the joy of my joys, the light of my life, the heart of my hearts – my everything. I look at you when you crawl into our bed at the crack of dawn and marvel at every single perfect thing about you.

I often say to your father that I would love to press 'pause' right now, as it doesn't seem that life could be any more perfect.

You are 10, eight and two, and all of you are showing signs of becoming exceptional people. You are kind, you are funny, you are polite and diligent, and you live with such a zest and hunger that I am sure you are destined for full and exciting lives.

I am happy that I can't press pause, though, as that would prevent me from seeing the wonderful young adults that you are becoming, boys, and the fierce, fearless, and feisty young girl that your little sister is growing into, thanks to your patience and protective guidance.

What a journey you have taken me on. Before I became a mother, I was convinced I would remain unchanged by motherhood. I was extremely career-oriented and a staunch feminist, and convinced I wasn't going to sacrifice my career or myself when I became a mother… until the doctor handed Barron to me and I felt his tiny body in my arms, and knew I was forever changed for the better.

Having you three children has completed me in an inexplicable way. You have given me my greatest purpose, my greatest love and my greatest joy. My heart is no longer mine, in the most glorious possible way, and now the three of you carry it entirely.

I don't think I have life figured out, but I have certainly learnt a lot along the way, most of it with the help of your amazing daddy. So my first bit of advice is to fall in love for the right reasons. Find someone who values you, who respects you and who is rooting for you. Find someone with whom you have a blast, who makes you laugh so hard your sides hurt. Your dad is all of these things to me and more, and that has made all the difference. Life will throw lots of curveballs at you, and having the right partner is invaluable for navigating the difficulties you will face.

Treat people kindly. We are at an extremely unsettling time politically, in a world where leaders are divisive, racist and intolerant. You have been raised in a privileged way and you must use this privilege to be kind to people and to do 'good' whenever you can.

With privilege comes responsibility, and it is your responsibility to treat people kindly and help those different and less fortunate than you, and I hope you will take this seriously, always. Do not judge anyone by their gender, the colour of their skin, their sexual persuasion or their background. I always remember the line from one of my favourite books, *To Kill a Mockingbird*, and would like you to remember it always, too: 'Never judge a man until you have walked a mile in his shoes.'

Respect women, always. They are the backbone of society, and your sister and I are the backbone of this family. Never underestimate the power of women. And please help me make sure that Wallis always loves and respects herself. Sadly, it is still not a given for young girls.

Do not look too much at what other people are doing. It is good to have a quick look, but then focus on yourself and what you are doing and where you are going. People project perfect lives on their iPhones – don't buy it. The most popular people on social media are among the dullest people I have met in my life. Likes on Instagram have nothing to do with likes or popularity in real life, so never confuse the two.

Please know how deeply you are loved, and let this bolster you always. Before your Nonna died, she always used to say to me that when she was gone, she would be an angel and would always be looking over me. I feel her always still, so please know there will never be a day when I am not there for you, looking over you and loving you.

I could write for days, but am surely making Barron cringe by now with all this sentimentality. I would like to leave with a quote from a letter Maya Angelou wrote to her younger self, and which I am passing on to you:

You're going to leave your mother's big comfortable house and she won't stop you, because she knows you too well.

But listen to what she says:

"When you walk out of my door, don't let anybody raise you — you've been raised.

You know right from wrong.

In every relationship you make, you'll have to show readiness to adjust and make adaptations.

Remember, you can always come home.

You will go home again when the world knocks you down — or when you fall down in full view of the world. But only for two or three weeks at a time. Your mother will pamper you and feed you your favourite meal of red beans and rice. You'll make a practice of going home so she can liberate you again — one of the greatest gifts, along with nurturing your courage, that she will give you.

Be courageous, but not foolhardy.

Walk proud as you are."

And know that you can always come home to me and Daddy. I love you, Barron, Snowdon and Wallis. Be courageous but not foolhardy, and always walk proud.

Your loving Mother

LAURA FANTACCI

CO-FOUNDER of WARDROBE ICONS
Mother to GRETA ZITA and VERA GILDA

An Italian in London, who began her career as the late Isabella Blow's fashion assistant on Tatler, *Laura made her name in 2007, when she launched her blog,* Wearing It Today, *or WIT, as it became known. She was working as fashion editor at* Red *magazine, but, when Greta Zita was a year old, Laura decided to focus on her blog full-time. Now in its fourth year,* Wardrobe ICONS, *Laura's digital shopping platform and online magazine, offers timeless style solutions for the modern woman.*

"Becoming a mother has made me accept imperfection in a way I didn't know possible," says Laura. "It softened me, it taught me to pick my battles and to constantly check myself. Having a child is like having a little witness, always watching if you lose your patience or do the things you tell them not to. It inspires you to be the best version of yourself."
In honour of the first shoot she did as a new mother – one of the first stories that ever ran on *The Grace Tales* – Laura has written a letter especially to her firstborn, Greta Zita.
"When Greta asks me, 'Why do you have to go to work?' I say to her, 'For two reasons: one, I really like my job.' I always compare it to the things she loves doing, like when she is absorbed in drawing or playing with friends," explains Laura. "'And two, so that we can afford all the nice things we have.' I don't say, 'I'm so sorry, I wish I could be with you.' That's not how I want her to perceive work. I don't want her to view it as suffering: I want her to find a job that she loves as much as I do."

"Amore, e' una bimba!"

It's with these four words that you came into my life, with your big, wide-open, almond-shaped eyes, looking at me in complete silence. You didn't cry for hours, to the point that your daddy and I were almost worried about you. You screamed a lot soon thereafter and, just like that, within the space of a moment between existing only in my imagination and being in my arms, on 14 September, 2014, at 2.33am, I became a mother, and you turned my life upside down in a way I never, ever imagined possible. Your daddy and I looked at you and said, "She will be called Greta Zita."

When we took you back home, I knew nothing about being a mother; nothing about selflessness, putting someone else first at all times and being in constant demand. I also knew nothing about that gut-wrenching love I would start to feel for you which would never stop; the love that almost haunts me in the constant fear of your existence being in jeopardy.

The first few months were tough. I felt inept and exhausted, because you may become a mother in a space of a moment, but you never stop learning how to be one. This is something I will attempt to prepare you for as you grow up. I may very well be unsuccessful at it, because one thing is true – nothing can prepare you for the shift in life when you become a mother for the first time. Yet hear this: despite all its challenges, the sleep deprivation and round-the-clock demands, I wouldn't change any part of you or our journey together for the world. I will love you, to the moon and back, all around the world and more than words can say; unconditionally, for better, for worse, in sickness and in health for eternity.

Today, you are a thoughtful, sensitive, curious little girl. You love your family, your irreplaceable daddy and your chatty little sister. You draw beautifully, are ambitious and always try your best. You love to laugh but can also be surprisingly deep and have sophisticated thoughts that are well beyond your five years. What I love most about you are your loyalty and fairness – you are just and will make a great friend one day, perhaps a wife and mother, too.

I sometimes worry about your sensitive side, that you care too much about what other people think of you; but I hope to help you build up the confidence to be your own person. For your future, I wish for you to feel capable and included, to know your potential, trust yourself and always be kind to everyone. As for me… you make me want to be a better person, to inspire you and make you proud. I hope one day you will talk about me in the total conviction that I have always tried my best. I will be forever grateful to you for the tumultuous journey you are taking me on. I know it won't be perfect; I know there will be times you will come to resent me, question my love, my judgment, even my commitment towards you.

But the day you do, there are two things I want you to remember. The first is that every decision I have taken in my life since you were born has been with the ultimate aim of being a present and supportive mother for you and your sister. The second is that you've made my life worthwhile. Nothing would make sense without you and your sister in it. Becoming your mother has defined me and given my life its ultimate purpose and meaning.

I love you, *tutto intorno al…* Mamma

PIPPA HOLT

DESIGNER / Mother to BAY, BALTHAZAR and ATTICUS

With a sunshine state of mind, a love of far-flung travel and a sharp eye for style, former British Vogue *editor and fashion consultant Pippa Holt wouldn't let a little thing like three children under the age of three stand between her and launching a new business, Pippa Holt Kaftans.*

Family life has never dampened Pippa's desire for adventure – Morocco, New York, Paris, Istanbul, Mykonos and Spain were just a handful of the places she visited while pregnant with her youngest son, Atticus. But it was a move to Houston, Texas, that sparked the desire to launch a namesake holiday collection of her own. Galvanised by happy childhood memories of fossicking on Australia's beaches, and her grandmother, Dame Zara Holt's tropical-inspired clothing on holidays at the Great Barrier Reef, she took a textile research trip to Mexico with her husband, Irish businessman Conor Roche. There, in a remote village, she met a weaver, Felipa, and her daughter, Angelica… The kaftans that Pippa subsequently wore through the heat of a Texas summer were the inspiration for her own eponymous range. These meticulously handmade, hand-loomed pieces are perfect for travel, the beach or simply relaxing at home. After spending some time living in Dublin, Pippa and her family have now returned to make their home in Sydney. "I'm still enjoying the smallness of my children, even the chaos they create," she says. "They are very close in age, so they need me around. I know this phase won't last, so I'm relishing it while doing my work in a way that allows me to be close to them. For that, I feel very fortunate."

Dear Bay, Balthazar and Atticus,

Your dad and I have tried to create a loving and secure childhood for you all, one from which you feel you have a strong foundation to grow, to flourish and become individuals. I hope you have wonderful memories of life and our global travels; of happy weekends filled with simple joys, like learning how to ride bikes in Rushcutters Bay Park with the Harbour Bridge in the distance; of hot Christmases in Australia and snowy ones in Ireland.

I hope you'll remember the beauty, fun and specialness of both places and the friends you've made. You have strong family connections in both Dublin and Sydney, and a community in each home.

I grew up in Melbourne and had a wonderful upbringing, going to the same school from beginning to end. I had creative, kind, loving parents, and my grandmother, Dame Zara Holt, was a huge influence on me. She told me to be "beautiful inside and out", and I teach the same to the three of you. Through her houses in Portsea and Far North Queensland, she showed me the tropics and the magnificence of Australia's coastline with all its wonders – from coral and shells, to snorkelling and the tides. Zarie was a true original.

I strive to be a kind, loving, patient mother who is present; one who is always there for her children, no matter what; one who gives you joy, as well as security. I hope you'll remember me for being kind, creative, loving, original and supportive, with a sense of fun.

Bay and Balthazar, I can already see your creativity growing. You do extra art lessons each week, love to design kaftans for me and we have easels and art stations set up in the house. We take sketchbooks to Sydney's Nielsen Park and when we travel abroad. I am often pointing out things I think we should draw, and you love that.

Life seems to be going so fast. Atticus, you are three and a half, and suddenly you are a little boy. It makes me a little nostalgic, but that is all part of life and how it moves forward. When you were born, the three of you were all under three years old and I found it overwhelming at times – harder, actually, than when I was mother to two babies born 14 months apart and we arrived in Texas in the hottest weather I have ever experienced. That was a challenge, but the hard work eventually rewarded me in the most amazing ways and I adored that phase of my life.

When I first became a mother, I took a step back from my career. I was still a contributing editor for British *Vogue* and continued to work for the magazine on projects. I was based in Dublin, so I was able to focus on my new role as a mother, and I am so pleased I did.

I have so many great memories of my 20 years' working in the fashion industry. When I started at *Vogue* Australia, I assisted fashion editors such as Judith Cook, Victoria Collison and Jillian Davison, who inspired me and taught me incredible things with their skill and great taste. I am still inspired today by what I learnt from those women in my early 20s. My first job in London was at the iconic boutique Browns. There, I learnt some fashion wisdom from the renowned Mrs Bernstein. Then, as the PR for clothing chain Whistles, I learnt from founder Lucille Lewin, who was clever enough to discover people like Dries Van Noten. The designer there at the time was Louise Trotter, who is so talented and remains an inspiring friend. Lisa Armstrong was the most amazing boss, and I worked for her at *The Times* for five years. She took me to fashion shows and opened up a whole new world for me. At 26 years old, I was styling a shoot a week and worked non-stop at the newspaper. I loved it.

At *Vogue*, I witnessed true talent like Lucinda Chambers, Kate Phelan and Fiona Golfar, and was lucky to have nine years there that I cherished every day. It was a real community of girls and we were like a family. Editor-in-chief Alexandra Shulman was a visionary leader and I admired her so much.

Since launching my business, there have been many highlights: a pop-up at Bergdorf Goodman in New York; launching on Net-A-Porter; featuring in American *Vogue*; partnering with matchesfashion. com on the launch of children's kaftans; and, best of all, seeing women around the world loving and wearing Pippa Holt Kaftans.

In my early 30s, my mother taught me "to thine own self be true", which I benefited from greatly, and I think it's a valuable lesson to learn from teenage years onwards. My mother, father and half-sister, Sophie Holt, all like to work hard. My father is 81 and still chooses to work. I think it's fulfilling, and self-discipline and dedication instilled when growing up helps. I hope you'll all carry on this trait and I will try to instil it. I've always told you to work hard at school to give you the freedom to achieve your dreams; to know that you can strive to be whatever you want to be when you grow up.

The love I have for you all is so strong. It's fulfilling in every way. You are my everything.

Love, Mum

> "I strive to be a kind, LOVING, patient mother who is PRESENT, one who is ALWAYS THERE for her children, no matter what..."

SOPHIE KEEGAN

JEWELLERY DESIGNER / Mother to MAX, CASPER and ALFIE

Born to an English father and Australian mother, Sophie began her life in London and later moved to Sydney with her parents, whose wanderlust triggered her abiding passion for art and design.

She studied painting in London, before training as a goldsmith and gemologist, then moved to Paris in 1993 to work with Chaumet in the Place Vendôme. There, she honed her craft alongside master goldsmiths and assisted in the creation of new lines for the store. Inspired, Sophie returned to London to launch her own label and open a boutique in Notting Hill. She was also commissioned to design a special piece for Hermès and collaborated with the venerable English company, Asprey.
With an aesthetic influenced by her family's love of the sea – they spend their summers sailing in Europe – Sophie has forged her reputation with a signature collection of elegant diamond-set 'Letters' necklaces. She now lives between Germany and Australia with her husband, Tino, and their three sons.

Dear Max, Casper and Alfie,

You are growing up a bit like I did, on two sides of the globe, which can be heart-wrenching at times. But it's wonderful that you can experience two very different cultures as you grow up. We've been so lucky to be able to divide our life between Germany and Australia for good amounts of time, and you've all made special connections and experiences in both places.

I was born in London to an Australian mother and an English father. When I was five years old, we moved to Sydney. I remember the long, hot Australian summer holidays spent on the beach in our 'cossies', running from beach house to beach house at Port Willunga in South Australia. I also have beautiful memories of white Christmases spent in England with my grandmother, aunts, uncles and 14 English cousins!

When I was 11, my parents moved to Singapore. I loved this chapter of our life, as it was my first taste of a new and exotic culture. However, Sydney's Watsons Bay always felt like our family home. Your grandparents still live in the same house today, and I cherish being able to share all these memories with you.

Your dad grew up in Hamburg, an elegant European city with a beautiful lake in the centre. You'll always remember this lake because you've all learnt to sail on it. Your dad is a keen sailor and we spend the European summers on our family boat. In the winter, we retreat to our holiday home in Switzerland and spend time together skiing. We've been on these holidays with you every year since you were born and I think it's beautiful that you will have these memories to treasure.

Max, you were my first and, after you arrived, I was so happy to be a mother. I took a huge step back from the busy life I had been leading in London to really focus on motherhood. It was an extremely challenging time of my life, as well. Your auntie – my dear sister – passed away just two months before I gave birth. She had been through the pregnancy with me, but never got to meet you all. If I could turn back the clock, it would be so that my lovely sister, Louise, could have held my baby in her arms. At that time of my life, the birth of my first child and the incredible love from your dad helped in the healing and recovery from the loss of my sister.

I want you all to know that life is all about what you make of it yourself. To have a passion for something and work hard at it, and to be an independent thinker are all so important. You must learn from your mistakes and understand how to handle rejection and take criticism, as these tools will just make you stronger.

I feel so lucky to have chosen a creative career. It really suits my lifestyle and it's wonderful how I can combine it with family life. I love to gather inspiration for my jewellery while I travel and always carry a sketchbook and pens with me in all my handbags. When I was just starting out and living in Paris, it was such a dream to work with the beautiful old jewellery house of Chaumet. I was only 23 and fresh out of design school. I walked every day from the 6th arrondissement across Paris and felt like I was living my dream.

I love nature and it has always inspired me in my work. You have all helped design pieces of jewellery for me, and I keep all your designs and drawings close to my heart.

You love your dad so much. He has been very hands-on from day one. You were all born via caesarean and, through each birth, he sat by me holding my hand. Afterwards, he lay with you on his chest, while I was still in the operating theatre. Those moments are still so close to my heart and have made my love for him stronger than ever.

Our lives have changed forever having you three beautiful boys. Every day, you bring more love, new challenges, wonderful surprises and so much joy that I could never have imagined.

Love, Mum

JULIE MONTAGU

YOGA INSTRUCTOR, NUTRITIONIST and MINDFULNESS GURU
Mother to EMMA, JACK, WILLIAM and NESTOR

To say there's more than meets the eye when it comes to Viscountess Hinchingbrooke is an understatement. Growing up in Illinois, USA, before moving to London and the breathtaking Mapperton manor house in Dorset (claimed as the finest in England by Country Life*), Julie Montagu epitomises the power of staying positive in the face of adversity.*

The one-time reality star – Julie had a brief stint on *Ladies of London* – is married to Luke Montagu, Viscount Hinchingbrooke, a down-to-earth aristocrat who is slowly rebuilding his life after a long-term health issue. The couple divide their time between their terrace in London and the family estate in Mapperton, where mindfulness, meditation and yoga play a significant role in their daily routine of work and kids. The wellness advocate and cookery writer is the author of three international bestselling books – *Superfoods*, *Eat Real Food* and *Superfoods, Superfast* – and *Recharge: A Year of Self-Care to Focus on You*, published last year. She is also known as 'The Flexi Foodie' through her website, which features yoga courses, healthy recipes, self-care advice and nutrition tips. Indeed, Julie couldn't be a finer example of the positive impact these all have on mind, body and soul.

To my four children, Emma, Jack, William and Nestor,

Well, you're nearly all grown up now and, truthfully, I used to wish for the day when you were! And now? Well, I want you back to the young age of destruction, temper tantrums, waking me up in the night, crying, being sick, and when you *all* believed in Santa Claus.

Oh, and when you all needed *me* too!

When you were younger, I had the bad habit of telling you that this was the first time I'd ever done this parenting thing and if I messed up, I'd pay for your therapy. So far, none of you has asked for that! Perhaps I've done it right?

But really, what is 'the right way' with parenting? I'm still figuring it out and will until I'm no longer able to parent you... But I took advice from my mom, your grandmother, a wonderful mother of five herself. Emma, when you were first born, she said, "Don't read a single parenting book – just do what comes naturally and what you think is right." So, I trusted her – she was, after all, my mom – and I thought I turned out ok.

And she was right. You four are all different – I had two of you in my 20s and two of you in my 30s – meaning I was different at each of your births. So, I did what I felt was right back then – individually – for all four of you. Yes, my parenting was pretty much the same for you all, *but* I did tweak it a bit based on each of your individual needs and personality.

I cherish the moments we all had – the good and the bad. Because if life – if parenting – were all good, it would be pretty darn boring. Take the good with the bad: the sleepless nights with the cuddling in bed the next morning; the vomiting and high fevers with the neediness and attachment staying home from school; the not-winning the-sports-day-race with the huge smile when spotted in the sea of parents at assembly; the heartbreak of losing with the triumph of winning.

As a parent, I wanted to be your biggest cheerleader – *no matter what*. Glass half-full; positivity over negativity always wins. That, my four kids, is the true meaning of winning – finding the silver lining in every dark cloud, the bright light in the midst of a dark forest. It's always there – you just have to never give up. Keep looking, find it and cherish the memories.

Because it's the memories and the people – not the things – that bring true happiness. I hope I leave a legacy through my parenting to you all. Just like my mom did. And I hope you know how much I love each and every one of you. You four complete me.

Love, Mom

SOPHIA WEBSTER

LUXURY ACCESSORY DESIGNER / Mother to BIBI BLOSSOM

Since her eponymous shoe brand launched in 2012, British designer Sophia Webster's whimsical creations have been described as the closest shoes can get to confectionery, and as hard to resist. Sophia recently opened her second London store, complete with a beauty salon, and lounge dedicated to bridal appointments. Since the birth of her daughter, Bibi Blossom, she's extended her collection to include children's shoes. She also recently became a mother to twins.

Sophia studied at the prestigious Cordwainers College, part of the London College of Fashion, then graduated from the Royal College of Art in 2010. She went on to be awarded the 2012 Condé Nast Footwear Emerging Designer of the Year, received the 2013 British Fashion Award for Emerging Accessories Designer, and won the British Fashion Council's (BFC) New Gen Award for her first three consecutive seasons. She has since won the coveted BFC *Vogue* Fashion Fund in 2016, becoming the first female shoe designer ever to be awarded this prize.

Dear Bibi Blossom,

You're the funniest, sassiest, most entertaining little lady I could ever imagine having the pleasure to raise. You constantly surprise me with your funny Bibi-isms and the way you see the world.

I love watching you play, especially your purist approach to dress-up. If you choose your Snow White costume, you need the wig, the shoes and before you put it on, you check with me that we have apples! Otherwise, it's not worth doing – right? You'll take one bite out of the apple, then collapse to the floor just like Walt Disney planned it. I usually sit and eat the rest of the apple, watching you in awe, thinking surely any three-year-old who takes fancy dress this seriously is destined for an Oscar one day.

I love lying in bed hearing you wake up in the morning. Sometimes, you start singing to yourself, which makes me and Daddy laugh. I lie there knowing that, in under a minute, depending on how you slept, you will bound in noisily or shuffle in, cocooned in your favourite blanket.

When you were two, you used to come in, crawl under the covers and say sleepily "Mornin', darlin'" to me in your little cockney accent, which simultaneously would crack me up and melt my heart. What has always amazed me is how you wake up every morning with Hollywood hair, as though you've had a full-on bouncy blow-dry. You have absolutely no idea how lucky you are!

You are a spirited, enthusiastic and excitable little sweetheart. You walk into a park and scan for potential friends, then stride up to them asking if they want to play with you. You are such a cutie that you usually get the answer you wanted. It breaks my heart to think that one day, someone could chip away at that confidence. Please don't let them!

You are such a force – fiercely independent, strong-willed, and you know your own mind, which I love. Whether you're zipping up your coat or peeling the lid off a yoghurt pot, you don't want any help. Instead, you whisper a little chant to yourself really fast: "I can do it, I can do it, I can do it, I can do it... *I did it!*"

Keep chanting, Bibi. Even when you're grown-up, keep believing in yourself. Be your own biggest cheerleader!

Always remember, your body is precious. Cherish it, even the bits you might not like. I didn't like my nose growing up, but I like it now. It's the same nose as your great-grandma Ruth's. She was a Czech refugee and had to be brave in a way we will never understand, so now when I look in the mirror I'm proud of this nose!

You inherited my chubby feet. I'm sorry for that! But my experience of these feet is that they can dance like Beyoncé, they can backflip, somersault and jump really far. Whatever you do with yours, please use them to stand your ground. I'll always be standing just behind you if you need me.

This is an exciting month for you, my lovely girl! You turned four last week. You start 'big school' this week and you are due to become a big sister next week! Your little world is about to experience some big changes, but I want you to know that whatever happens and however tall you grow, you will always, always be my baby.

These twin girls in my tummy will be very lucky to have such a smart, kind and brave big sister like you. I worry about the responsibilities of raising three girls. How will I teach you all that you are enough just the way you are? That whatever you are going through that feels insurmountable today will not feel so bad in a few days' time. I want you to be safe and streetwise and not take too many risks. If you do take a risk, make sure it is you who decides. Never do something you're uncomfortable with just because your friends are doing it.

You can't control all the events that will happen to you, but you can control how you let them affect your life. My dad always said, "You win some, you lose some, kid," and he was right. Some things are going to go your way, some things are going to turn your whole world upside down, but you must always be *resilient*!

My world did just that last year when my dad, your beloved Grampi, left his house to go to the sports centre and never came home again. You were two at the time, his only precious grandchild, and it makes me sad that the special relationship you had was so short-lived. His attacker is in prison now, but that doesn't feel like justice. All we have is the hope that one day he will regain full consciousnes, his damaged brain will make new connections and he will learn to walk and talk again. Some say we're being unrealistic, but what do we have if we don't have hope? Hope is a wish, and its strength is the strength of your desire.

I hope you live a life you are proud of and have the courage to change anything that doesn't feel right. Do not settle. Do not settle for a relationship with a partner who doesn't encourage your dreams. Your Daddy believed in mine and we built a business, a family and a life together that we are thankful for every day, and we did it on our own terms.

I believe that to get anywhere in life you should only rely on yourself, your talent and your tenacity. You are not owed or entitled to anything from the world just for being you. I will be here to support and encourage you always, but the drive and determination can only come from inside you.

You asked me last week, "Can I be the Queen when I grow up so I can be the boss of everyone in the land?" I told you in theory you could, but you'd probably have to marry Prince George first. You said you can't do that because you're going to marry Daddy. We agreed instead that you should be prime minister, in charge of all the rules!

Since that conversation, you have announced to everyone that when you grow up you are going to be the 'Rhyme Minister', which sounds like a pretty inspired name for a rapper! So Miss Bibi, whether you want to be a politician, a royal or a rap star, the future is yours to create, my angel.

You are loved my baby girl, fiercely and forever.
Mummy x

ELISE PIOCH

FOUNDER of MAISON BALZAC / Mother to LOULOU

If you've always thought there's just something about French women, wait until you meet Elise Pioch. Not only is this former fashion buyer utterly stylish, her honesty and unruffled attitude to business and motherhood are utterly disarming. It's all part of Elise's charm – to tell it like it is, while maintaining a lighthearted approach to everything she does.

Elise spent 13 years in Australia, where she and her husband, Pablo, divided their time between a beautifully restored church on the Hawkesbury River and a warehouse space in Sydney. Her range of beautiful, evocative scented candles – inspired by her own childhood memories of life in the south of France – has now expanded to include heavenly scents, mouth-blown glassware and ceramics.
The lure of these happy memories and an abiding connection with her family heritage have now brought Elise and her family back to France.

"*My CHILDHOOD was so unbelievably HAPPY that I wanted you to get a GLIMPSE of it and choose your FAVOURITE pieces to make your OWN PUZZLE.*"

Dearest Loulou,

For the past few years, we spent our time between the Maison Balzac warehouse in Botany and our church home in the country. Your favourite thing to do was to pick feijoa fruits and sit down in the grass together and peel the hard skin to reveal the pale pink, sweet flesh.

I hope you will remember every animal we had in Australia: the chickens, Ben and Holly; your cat, Chacha (a gift from us to you when you turned three); and the goanna that used to live under our house.

I know you will remember your first best friends, Daisy and Marilou. You seem to be very loyal, and care so much for your friends that sometimes you cry, saying you are scared something could happen to them and you won't be there for them now we live in France.

I think you will also remember your new life in the South of France, feeling very far from the country of your birth and missing your morning swims in the ocean. I hope that you will come to appreciate the benefits of our move, such as being fluent in French and having access to both cultures, as well as having spent time with your grandparents, uncles, aunts and cousins.

If I'm honest, I was extremely scared about falling pregnant. I didn't think I could ever give birth and thought I'd be the worst mother on Earth. When I discovered I was expecting a baby, I was frightened, but your dad held me tight and said we could do this together. You are the result of the passionate love I have for him.

So we dived together into this adventure and I am so happy we did. I adored being pregnant with you. I had the most natural and uneventful birth: I breathed for 12 hours in a hot bath and there you were – healthy and so small! It took me a good 24 hours to realise I was the mother of you – a very small baby. Then I gave you a big kiss, and this was the bond I will always remember.

Right now, life in France is still only beginning. But so far it is delicious, family-driven and different from what I remembered! Life in Australia was friendly, easy, optimistic, but far away from family and my origins. Not one day goes by without you asking, "When are we going back to Australia, Mama?" And every time it makes me question our choice. As long as we three are together as a family, then I feel that we have made the right choices and are moving forward as a strong team.

I am trying to create a childhood filled with good memories of places, people, smells, ideas and culture. My childhood was so unbelievably happy that I wanted you to get a glimpse of it and choose your favourite pieces to make your own puzzle. I truly believe that if your childhood is made of a few strong, simple things, then you can build a strong, simple life on top of it.

I constantly remind you that all dreams are achievable. I don't want you to put any limits on your imagination; instead, I want you to surprise us by how much you can achieve just by making your dreams a reality.

When I first became a mother, I felt I was completely losing my freedom. Not having a break for the first year really put me in a bad place: I was exhausted, depressed... In my darkest hours, I would walk barefoot in the garden at night, crying to the sky and stars to help me.

My grandmother once told me that when people are not around and you still want to speak to them, you can do so through the stars. I always felt calmer after that, and maybe it helped me, too.

I had to go back to France for a few months to be looked after by my parents. I never fully recovered from that burn-out and I still cannot multitask as much as I used to. Motherhood changes us for life, in bad and good ways, but I've learnt to accept it.

> *"Since I gave birth, I feel a deep CONNECTION to all females... to HUMANITY."*

I have so much respect for all the mothers out there. I now understand what my grandmother and mother did for me, and what other women go through. Since I gave birth, I feel a deep connection to all females. It has connected me to humanity in a way that's changed my life. I can never feel alone again.

I started Maison Balzac one month before falling pregnant; there was never a question of me stopping my career while raising you. I've always followed my dreams, and my focus and determination have taken me exactly where I wanted to be and beyond. My pursuit for the rare and beautiful made me have you, the most rare and beautiful person I know.

Remember there are two things necessary in life: failure and the ability to say no. Both will lead to better solutions, better outcomes and more humble paths. Small children can't cope with failure; it is painful to watch! But by reminding them that play involves winning and losing, I believe they will slowly understand failure.

I cannot wait to hear all the ideas, projects and dreams you will come up with. You are continuously pushing the boundaries of cuteness and I wonder, can I love you more than I do today? You have decided to become a vet and run a zoo at the same time, so imagine how impatient we are to see if you do exactly that or if you choose to be a magician or a candlemaker.

You are the biggest surprise and gift of my life. You showed me I was stronger than I thought and connected me to humanity in a way that I didn't know existed.

Merci, ma Loulou, Maman (qui t'aime)

DIANA WATSON

ARTIST / Mother to PENELOPE, FELICITY and BRIGITTE

"Never let a chance go by... youth is not eternal." "Living near the water inspires such possibility." These are the kind of lovely words that linger in your mind after you visit Diana Watson, one of Australia's most talented painters. The 73-year-old mother of three is full of wonderful reflections on life and she's the kind of woman with whom you could happily talk for hours.

After visiting Diana's charming Kirribilli apartment on the edge of Sydney Harbour, filled with her spectacular oil-on-canvas paintings, your curiosity may lead you to wonder how it all began. Given her success over the past decade – her painting, *Bed of Roses*, found its way to Hollywood on the set of film *Collateral Beauty*, starring Kate Winslet, Helen Mirren and Will Smith; and her largest mural to The Palm hotel in Dubai – it's surprising to discover that she didn't wholly pursue her career until after her three daughters had left home. In fact, Diana didn't started painting professionally until the age of 50. Diana is also a grandmother to seven children.

To my three wonderful daughters, Penelope, Felicity and Brigitte,

Thank you for the gift of motherhood. Whatever would I do without you? As adults, you have become my best friends and given me seven amazing young people, our grandchildren. Watching over you, from birth to becoming mothers yourselves, has been joyous. If there were any heartaches or worry, I have blissfully forgotten those moments. They were only moments...

I have often thought that I no longer need to give you advice unless you ask for it. I give you credit for having your feet firmly planted on the ground and that the life decisions you make are the best.

When you all left school, it was amazing to find we had the same interests. Our conversations revolved around every aspect of design and food. It wasn't surprising when the eldest of you became an architect, the second, a paediatric dietician and the youngest, the designer of an 'it' handbag that is sold worldwide. Naturally, we are more than proud of you.

The only way to learn about life and parenting is from your own parents. This statement comes with a warning. Being a parent is the greatest, most important responsibility we ever face. It is about setting an example and being consistent, with love as well as discipline. If we live metaphorically untidy lives, our children will not know any better. The reply to this is that we have choices.

My parents and I lived on a horse stud at the foot of the Darling Ranges. It was an idyllic life and I did not miss having siblings until my parents were in their final years. My childhood memories are of my paternal grandfather, an old gold miner, who loved horses and always had peppermints in his pockets – for them and me.

Our house was surrounded by fig and almond trees. We had an orchard of citrus fruit and peaches, and a big old mulberry tree in the middle of a stallion yard. Needless to say, I spent a lot of time sitting in trees and eating whatever was in season. We had a dairy farm next door and a billy of milk was hung on the fence for us every morning. It must have been the best diet for a small child.

I don't think my parents had to face many problems with an only child. As far as I remember, they never had to discipline me; I knew there were boundaries. I always felt loved, but never spoilt. Boarding school from eight years

old taught me about never questioning rules and living with a whole lot of girls; about self-discipline, punctuality and respect. I made friends I would have for the rest of my life. And as I grew up, the one thing that kept me on the straight and narrow was that I could never disappoint my father; I had too much love and respect for my parents.

After a brief career in advertising, I married when I was 20 years old and became a mother at 22. I don't remember even holding a baby until I was handed my first little girl. Ignorance was bliss; I found that doing what came naturally (with advice from Dr Spock, the only self-help book of the time) seemed to work. Of course, there was a mothercraft nurse to help when we got home, and the 'new father', who was a surprising mine of information.

I confess that a library book was my secret weapon for breastfeeding. It made for a relaxed mother and a happy baby. There were certain stresses in being a stay-at-home mother, but the consolation was that most of my friends were in the same boat.

Staying home to care for the family seemed like an overdose of domesticity. However, our groceries were delivered by a gentleman wearing a shirt and tie; there was a dear old baker the children called 'Toast'; a lady with a car-load of library books. Everything was at our doorstep.

I always had a creative project on hand, from *trompe l'oeil* painting to wedding dresses, but finally the right time came for me to restart my career. It now seems I am 'driven' and I feel so fortunate to have my art, something I love doing that fills every day.

This year, it seems you are all spreading your wings. As one of you said, "I don't want to die wondering." We are so happy to see you all following your dreams. Remember, your forebears came from the UK and the mountains of northern Italy in the mid-1800s. Their sense of adventure is part of who you are today.

An old Italian friend told me that a woman must have a passion in her life aside from the love of her husband and family. For me, this is my painting, and something I will have in my life forever. So girls, there is life after children and, rather than feeling obsolete and invisible, you will have a new *raison d'être*.

With all my love, Mum

> *"I give you credit for having your feet FIRMLY PLANTED on the ground and that the LIFE DECISIONS you make are the best."*

AMANDA BOOTH

MODEL, ACTRESS and ADVOCATE / Mother to MICAH

*If you follow LA-based Amanda Booth on Instagram (@amanda_booth),
you would have already fallen in love with her beautiful son, Micah Quinones
– not to mention been blown away by her strength and courage.*

Before Amanda gave birth, she discovered Micah's heartbeat was faint.
"This is what led us down that dark rabbit hole. His heart looked great, but that's
when they said his other measurements were not so good. He was very small.
Words like achondroplasia or intrauterine growth restriction were thrown
around. We had the foetal non-stress test multiple times a week, until finally
he wasn't doing so well, so I had to be induced at hospital."
When Micah was four months old, he was diagnosed with Down syndrome.
"I have tons of advice for mothers of babies with Down syndrome," says Booth.
"First, that it's ok to be sad or worried, to mourn the loss of the life you envisioned
for you and your child. It is going to be different, yes. But that does *not* mean that
it will be less, in any way! We try not to treat Micah any differently. If we don't,
then I think we have a better shot than others doing the same thing."

Dear Micah,

I hope you go through life loving yourself as much as I love you. You've given me a sense of purpose that I've never felt before. You've opened my eyes. You've taught me the importance of equality, inclusion and acceptance, and how to fight for someone other than myself. Every single day, you teach me to slow down and be present in the moment.

I grew up in Pennsylvania. My own childhood was very challenging, but now I appreciate all the struggles I had to endure at a young age. They not only shaped me into the person I am today, but also into the kind of parent I wanted to be. My parents divorced when I was very young. There were a lot of addiction problems in our family, and we were always moving. Nothing really ever felt stable – there was definitely nothing beautiful or poetic about it. I grew up taking care of my younger siblings, and they saw me as a mother figure. My little sister – your auntie - would call me Mum all the time.

Your grandmother worked three jobs just to keep us afloat, so I never really had a close relationship with my parents, as they were so busy working. Yet, while your grandmother wasn't able to be hands-on with cooking dinner or helping me with homework, I was still able to observe her. I feel fortunate that, even as a young person, I could see the sacrifices she was making for us and I never had any resentment towards her.

Thirteen years ago, your grandmother moved in with me when I was living in New York City, and that's truly when our relationship-building began. Living together as adults, it was more of a friendship than it was the standard mother-daughter relationship. Your grandmother taught me to be a strong, independent woman; to work hard for the things I wanted and not to rely on a man or anyone else for them.

She also taught me that motherhood comes with a lot of personal sacrifices, but you'll be greatly rewarded when you have given a human a beautiful platform for a wonderful life and future. None of this she ever told me – I just knew from paying attention.

Your late great-grandmother was my role model. She did everything for her family. She worked 12 hours a day in a candy factory until the day of her open-heart surgery, which eventually led to her passing. She always made sure we had boots in winter, a warm meal on Sundays. She always made time for us kids and still worked her butt off. She had very little, but I never heard her complain, ever.

We found out you had Down syndrome when you were four months old. Towards the end of my pregnancy, things got complicated: I was on bed rest and a diet of 4000 calories a day to see if you would gain any weight.

You didn't; only I did, so we knew something was not functioning correctly. We had known about the possibility of you having Down syndrome from the day you were born, but it wasn't until the blood test confirmed it that we knew for sure. Your paediatrician came to our house to tell us.

I did mourn the loss of the life I'd envisioned for you – a 'barefoot on the beach' kind of childhood. At first, when you were diagnosed, you had seven therapy sessions a week, visits to the doctor, seemingly endless blood tests... It all felt very opposite to the life that I had imagined for you.

Now, you're four years old and we've gotten into the groove of navigating life, and your dad and I are trying to get back on track and give you the type of childhood we had hoped for.

One of the most incredible parts about parenting you is the indescribable joy we experience when you do something that any typical kid will do naturally. The other day, you said "pop" for popsicle and I just looked down and started crying – seeing you formulate a word was the most incredible feeling. We remember the first time you held some beads and dropped them; the first time you ate a tortilla chip and didn't choke because you figured out how to chew it and then swallow.

We get to experience the joy of you being proud of yourself when we ask you to do something and you do it. The smile you get on your face when you feel proud of yourself fills me with happiness.

I started modelling when I was 18. I drove back and forth between New York and Pennsylvania for two months until a modelling agency finally put me on their books. Most of them thought I was too old or too fat and, at that time, I had just turned 19. But I never gave up on myself.

That was 14 years ago, and it wasn't because somebody scouted me at the mall or because I was in the right place at the right time. It was because I had an idea of something that I wanted and I never gave up on myself. And I'm still here – modelling and acting – and I'm still not giving up on myself.

I hope, like me, you will have a go at everything and do it with as much passion and love as you possibly can. If it doesn't go your way, remember to let go. Something else is always around the corner; you just have to put one foot in front of the other.

I strive to be a far more patient mother to you than I feel. I hope you will never question how deeply I love you or how much I believe in you. I hope to be the kind of mother who slows down and looks at what you need, instead of what I need or what I think you need. I hope that I'm honest and that I can inspire other people to connect with their kids in ways they've never done before.

Micah, go through life with love in your heart. As I'm getting older, I'm realising that the more I nurture the relationships in my life, the happier I feel and the more purposeful my life feels.

Material things come and go, so it doesn't make sense to equate your life to things that could be taken away from you. It's better to put your energy into nurturing the things that no one can ever take away from you, and that's the love you give and the love you receive.

You are my heart.

With all my love, Mama

> "You've taught me the importance of EQUALITY, inclusion and ACCEPTANCE, and how to fight for someone other than myself."

CANNA CAMPBELL

FINANCIAL PLANNER, AUTHOR
and FOUNDER of SUGARMAMMA.TV / Mother to ROCCO

Spend a little time with Canna Campbell and you'll want to get out of bed at 5am, de-clutter your home and take charge of your finances. She has that effect on people – which is why her YouTube channel Sugar Mamma.TV *has attracted more than 100,000 loyal subscribers. She also runs financial planning business Sass Financial Australia.*

Canna's first book, *The $1000 Project,* is a guide to mindful saving and was published last year after she saved $32,000 in 12 months by using her unique strategy of bundling – saving and earning extra money in small, achievable parcels of $1000. Her favourite thing to do in the world is to walk along the beach with her five-year-old son, Rocco, partner Tom and two dogs, Giuseppe and Sophia.

To my little Monkey;

As I held you in my arms for the very first time, I was terrified about how to do this whole motherhood thing. Completely clueless. But I knew that you and I were a team, and that faith would help us figure out how to do it, somehow. And we did, and our bond is a testament to that.

It amazes me how much you have enriched my life and taught me patience, presence and perseverance. Taught me, also, that the things that really matter are those special bonds and simple routines, silly jokes and characters that we've created to help turn challenging situations into comical ones. It is the simplicity that has brought us our connection – from ending the day acknowledging our highlights, making burritos with Tom, secret chocolate waffles after school, and pant-wetting tickle fights on the sofa, to endless games of snakes and ladders, and cuddles through the night as you nestle in close to my heart.

As I watch your compassionate and gentle soul grow from a baby to a boy, I am proud and excited to see what your future holds. Your creative spirit, kindness and positive embracement of life are the foundations of your strength of character, so promise me you will never lose sight of these and remain true to yourself, centred and grounded.

Life will be full of challenges, but look for the wise lessons, embrace the journey unfolding ahead of you for strength, and follow your heart. Always try to take the higher path, as you will never regret this. Speak words of kindness and look for solutions when faced with difficult times. Be mindful of your tone as you speak aloud, and always remember that you win more bees with honey. Feel compassion for people who try to hurt you, as they are only hurting themselves. Care for and respect the environment, invest 10 per cent of every dollar you earn, and always eat your vegetables.

"I love you more than anything in the whole wide world... *ti voglio bene*."

xox Mamma

LAUREN HASTINGS

MODEL and ACTRESS / Mother to MONROE

Born in San José, California, Lauren Hastings grew up in the small town of Clovis. She's now based in LA, where she's raising her daughter, Monroe, as a single mother: "My advice to other single mothers is to have a really good support system and to try to take time for yourself," she says. "It's so important." Lauren's own mother, whom she still speaks to daily, taught her patience and unconditional love, and it's these traits, among many others, that she is now passing onto her own daughter.

Beginning your motherhood journey in the neonatal intensive care unit dealing with a life-and-death situation is something you'll never forget, and it's still an experience that brings tears to Lauren's eyes. Monroe was born at 26 weeks, when Lauren went into labour unexpectedly after a prenatal massage. She was hospitalised for more than four months and, when Monroe was finally brought home, she was on oxygen 24 hours a day, seven days a week and being fed though a gastrostomy tube. But, while it has been an experience Lauren will never forget, it has made her stronger. And, four years on, she's blessed with her happy, healthy little girl.

Dear Monroe,

I grew up in a small town in California called Clovis. We had a big backyard with a giant pool that had a rock waterfall and diving board. You would have loved it. I remember always being in the pool in the summer. We didn't live far from Yosemite National Park and lots of lakes, so I had a blast growing up. We had a lot of freedom and spent most days outdoors. Living in a small town felt so safe. I loved where I grew up.

I discovered I was pregnant when I was in Paris on a job for a fashion brand called The Kooples. I was scared and nervous, but most of all, I was so grateful and excited.

The early days after you arrived weren't typical of most mamas. You were born at 26 weeks, when I went into labour unexpectedly after a prenatal massage. You weighed two pounds and two ounces. So many of my memories of being a new mama were of spending them in the neonatal intensive care unit. There were many highs and many lows – not knowing whether you'd make it through the night was terrifying. I was scared, I was sad, I was terrified, I was angry – I was every emotion all at once. But I was strong, I was your protector, I was your mother.

There were a lot of moments that were scary. It was a life-and-death situation. I do remember always knowing that you'd be ok, and that, soon enough, you'd be home with me where you belonged. I coped by seeking support from my family and friends, taking it day by day and knowing that tomorrow would be new, different and exciting.

For a long time, I felt sad, guilty, ashamed and confused. I wondered why I couldn't protect you and keep you in my belly. Why couldn't I carry you? Why didn't you feel safe? Why did you come early? What was wrong with my body?

It was really hard. But you were a fighter and so is your mama.

It's true what they say – it all goes by so fast. You're four now. The first year after you arrived seemed a little longer and a bit more blurry, but after that, it sped up. It's exciting and a little heartbreaking at the same time. The other night, you were sleeping and I put my hand on the bottom of your feet and they were almost as long as my hand. I wanted to stop time right then. I wanted to hold on to that moment forever.

I also want to bottle your little laugh. You are so funny and you have such a quick sense of humour. And I adore your vivid imagination. You're constantly pretending to be a puppy named Sever, or a mummy who can't see, or a werewolf howling at the moon. You're so creative in play.

I strive to be a patient, soft and understanding mama. But also a mother who creates boundaries and sets good examples. Tough love, but not too tough. I try to encourage you to help solve

> "I want to TURN BACK time or pause it right where we are NOW... I hope you never stop wanting to CUDDLE."

problems and give you the tools to guide you through them. I want you to work hard for what you want. I want you to know that a woman can do anything and become anything she sets her mind to, that you can achieve your goals no matter how big they might be!

We co-sleep now and I feel so many things when you're sleeping: how big you've got, how long your legs are now; how you still sleep with your arms thrown up above your head like you did when you were a baby.

I want to turn back time or pause it right where we are now. You're still a toddler, but teetering on becoming a young girl, and it freaks me out and excites me all at once. I'll miss being able to carry you. I hope you never stop wanting to cuddle, or grabbing my face and telling me you love me before giving me tons of kisses.

I fear for kindergarten and how you'll adjust, even though that's a year away. It's a fear I never had before I had a child and a fear because of the climate we live in today. I try to replace the negative thoughts with the good ones. I know we're both so lucky!

The industries I chose as my career are modelling and acting, so I quickly got used to feelings of rejection and failure – they're part of life and I'll teach you that. But I also quickly learnt that clients have a particular look or image in their mind and you either fit the look or you don't – it's not personal. I've been in this profession since I was 12, so I've learnt to just leave those feelings at the door. I'm 34 now and genuinely feel comfortable and, for the most part, happy and content. I finally feel like I'm comfortable in my skin.

I'm a single mama, but one day I hope I meet 'the one'. I am so open to love. And I'm excited for the years ahead we have together: to be able to communicate with you more; you one day asking me for advice; watching you fall in love for the first time... I'm so excited to see you become a young lady. I love the now and I'm excited about everything to come.

Live a happy, joyous and free life. Save your money. Travel more in your 20s. Don't be so hard on yourself all the time. Stand by your beliefs and values, and know that being different is beautiful. Remember that success is feeling happy; it's not about how much money is in your bank account or having those new shoes on your feet. It's about inner happiness and inner calm. That's success to me. Ultimately, I want you to be genuinely happy and to love yourself as much as I love you.

Thank you, Monroe. Thank you for fighting so hard. Thank you for making every moment more meaningful and full of love. Thank you for choosing me to be your mama. I love you to the moon and back. I love you more every day. You have forever made me the happiest mama out there. You are my heart.

Love, Mom

ALEXANDRA ELLE

AUTHOR / Mother to CHARLEIGH and ILA

Alex Elle's words of affirmation have won the hearts of many, near and far. Whether through her books or empowering 'notes to self' shared on social media, the strength of sisterhood and women standing together are recurring central themes. Alex's candid, often vulnerable, words are infused with life lessons discovering self-love and caring for one's overall emotional wellbeing in the process.

When Alex was in her pre-teens and unable to fully communicate her feelings, her therapist recommended she write them down. Later, as a young, African American single mother, she began to write positive and uplifting messages to herself.
Alex now lives in Washington DC with her husband and two daughters. Her podcast, *hey, girl*, is dedicated to intimate conversations with other women about their personal tales. Her 10-year-old daughter, Charleigh, is a budding photographer. "Something I like to instil in my daughter is that being her best self is important," says Alex. "In all that she does in this life, I want her to know that she is allowed to show up confidently in all the spaces she occupies. Watching Char love herself and be herself is the greatest gift I've gotten as a parent."

To my daughters,

My hope for you, as you unfold to bloom and stretch your wings in this life, is that you explore every
corner of your journey with curiosity, compassion, and creativity. Be your own biggest cheerleader,
shout your worth from the rooftops, nurture your innermost desires. Play, grow and enjoy even the
hardest of times. Play some more. Find your freedom and bring it to fruition.

There will be many things on your path to wholeness that will frighten you; threaten to knock down what
you've built, even. But as you move through the world, own that you're fully capable of unfolding into
your best self, despite the obstacles. Each pivot of your path won't always be pretty. Some steps will
seem scarier than they really are, and some will prove to be hard to climb. Do not be swayed by
the turbulence that will arise; we've all experienced it. Trust and believe that there is magic within your
bones waiting for you. Unleash it. Unlock your mind and know deep in your heart that your journey
is worth it. Each high and low, ebb and flow is there to teach you something. Learn something when
you stumble. Find peace not only in the glory but also in the grit.

A deep wish that I have for you both is that you give yourself grace. Treat yourself like you would a best
friend, take your own good advice, make space for starting over. Don't shrink for the comfort of others.

Live out loud. Be big! Create heroes out of your dreams, move mountains and lift oceans with the
promise of tomorrow. You don't have to stay stuck or stay put. Spread your wings, dear ones. Don't allow
anyone to silence you, even your inner critic. Practise the ritual of being kind to yourself. Plant gardens
of hope, and let knowledge be your token. Never stop absorbing information, especially if it fascinates
you. Read lots of books. Ask questions. Draw. Paint. Write. Keep your imagination inspired. Be creative
and whole. Work for what you have and take care of it, whatever it is.

Listen to one another. Support each other as you walk your unique paths. Keep one another close.
Lean on each other. Sisterhood is a sacred bond that you two are blessed to have. Don't let your
anger get the best of you; it is fuelled by fear. Let love be louder, always.

Trust in yourself and your ability to fly, even when you think you'll fail. Regardless of the self-doubt you
may meet, understand that you are graceful, grand and brave. There is no need to hide from your truth.
What I have learnt in my life is this: failure is an option. If we don't fall, we don't learn to rise through
adversity. Choosing to learn from our missteps is where the triumph lies. Don't be afraid of your
potential. Be each other's mirror and love one another fiercely, just like you love yourself.

Love, Mom

INNIKA CHOO

DESIGNER and INFLUENCER / Mother to EADIE, MEIMEI and DANTE

"From the minute we wake, I'm blown around in a Choo gale-force whirlwind," says Innika Choo of her three children. "Any plans I might have had are re-routed like an out-of-date Google map. I'm a mess, but that's ok – it's a warm, good-vibe mess and somehow in the re-route, I'm quite happy to be lost among them."
The Australian-born, Bali-based mother's career journey kicked off on Instagram, where she quickly gained a following as much for her humour and honesty as her free-spirited aesthetic. In 2016, she launched her eponymous fashion label inspired by her life in Bali and love of vintage style.

"When I first had Eadie, pretty much all the mums I knew were full-time-working, super-hero-mum-jugglers; still functioning in the real world while dabbling in a bit of parenthood. Outstanding effort – I was in awe, but not able to keep up," says Innika. "Since then, I've had two more babies and now work full-time – my identity has morphed, again. The days were long and hard in those early years, but you never know at the time that they actually don't last forever. As my young ones have become little people, we've all matured into this life together (it's just that my knees are a bit more saggy than theirs)."

My darling Eadie, Meimei and Dante,

Well my loves, this one has been rather hard to pen. As I sit here to write, I find there's too much – too many feelings; too many complex knowing, loving, painful, thrilling understandings – for these mere words to cut it in a letter.

With every moment I see you smiling, I'm filled equally with a happiness that brings instant tears to my eyes and a squeeze of my heart that feels so good it almost hurts. I feel proud that I've managed to keep you happy until now, fear that one day you won't be so happy, and an urgency to keep you smiling, laughing, gurgling – whatever it is in that very moment of your simple happiness that has made you so joyful.

When you are profound and say the most clever things, my heart leaps in an almighty triumphant dance: "Hurrah, my child is clever!" Simultaneously, I worry I haven't taught you enough yet. I worry I'm not clever or disciplined enough to keep you making these profound, incredible statements.

When you are hurt (not so much the tripping-over hurt – the real emotional stuff, like when you fight with each other, when I hear for a fragment of a second your heart drop in pain), my heart goes for the ride, too, and I'm on my knees in front of you, fear in my eyes, wanting to fix everything.

I want to teach you everything, I want you to be able to sit on my shoulder and see everything from where I'm looking. I want you to know how incredibly loved you are (there must be a better word; 'love' doesn't seem strong enough).

I suppose I should try and simplify what I'm feeling as I try to type this, for the sake of getting all this layered emotion down; for the sake of you reading this to the end without wanting to wander off. My love for you three is big, and it's something I don't even know if you will really comprehend until maybe one day you feel it, too, with your very own little loves.

The three of you have been the making of me (I feel that such a tired cliché is no less true when I write it, and slightly disappointed that I have nothing more unique to say in its place). I would never have been compelled to do what we have in the past few years if it weren't for you.

I live in fear and anticipation for the teenage years, when you're even more profound and teach me things I never knew possible; when you open my eyes with your youthful, determined standpoints; and when your heartbreaks are truly heartbreaks that might last your lifetime. I live in fear of that pain. I pray that, perhaps in my lifetime, I might have had enough heartbreak and pain on the scale of woes that I've borne it all for you, and you'll just continue on this beautiful, happy trajectory forever.

Your dad and I, although very much in love, as you know, fight about most things, as you know. But ultimately, we are united about you three. We share our own love and companionship, but you are another bond that connects us. You are us.

I've made every mistake possible: I've been led down many garden paths, believed the wrong people, cared very deeply for the careless, invested my heartfelt time in the cruel. I've dabbled with the dark and I've been reckless with my purity. I am the woman I am for what I have lived.

But my heart twists in fear and elation, suspense – and always worry – with the thought that you are embarking on your own journeys into this life. And, indeed, it is sometimes a cruel, heartless world if you take a wrong turn. The exciting thing is that I've come this far with not much. So imagine how far the three of you will go with each other, backed up by the steadfast, reliable, consistent, unwavering (please help me find all the right words to express it) love your dad and I have for you.

You don't need much in this life. You will get by with a twinkle in your eye and a knack for dancing through open doors. For all the mistakes I've made along the way, at the very least, I've a very good story to tell. Opportunities are everywhere – there are kind people in the jungle, too. The problem is that the very same glowing traits that attract the kind people are the ones that cruel people tend to sniff out to rip you off. But shine brightly regardless, as I will be right there ready to take on anyone who tries. I'll be sure to tell you if something is off, if only you will trust my judgement. I just hope you live a life like mine but better, with a clever head on your shoulders and your dad and (silly but experienced) mum to join you for the ride from time to time. (We will embarrass you, and you need to be ok with that.)

I want you to cherish each other. I can see how much you care for one another so far and I wonder if, in my hopes for this to happen, I have forced you to be so close, or if it's beyond me and was in the stars that you were destined to share your lives together. Your relationships with each other will outlast every other relationship in your lifetime. You will know each other the longest. You will share memories and beautiful stories till the end of time. You will grow with one another. I'll be here for most of that ride, but your bond will outlast my lifetime, too, and that's the most thrilling thing about parenting.

I've come from a very social but somewhat lonely place to create beings who are my companions. But for you all to also be companions is the most wonderful thing. So cherish your friendship, please.

I love you (a mere word that cannot even begin to describe what I mean when I write it).
Your Mama xx

177

CAMILLA FREEMAN-TOPPER

CO-FOUNDER of CAMILLA AND MARC
Mother to LEUDICA, MISSY and WOLFIE

"I love what I do, but my family is my absolute number-one priority. What I've sacrificed is sleep, but I'm ok with that," says Camilla Freeman-Topper, one of the most recognised names in Australian fashion. She founded CAMILLA AND MARC with brother Marc Freeman in 2003, and they've grown it into one of the country's most successful luxury fashion brands.

Known for their timeless, elegant 'forever pieces', the duo's aim has always been to enrich women's lives through their designs. Camilla is ample proof that with a little organisation, a good work ethic and getting your priorities straight, you can have the best of both worlds – a thriving business and happy, contented children.

A letter to Leudica, Missy and Wolfie,

I always knew I wanted you. I feel so lucky I met your father at a young age and settled down so I could become a young mum. We both wanted the same thing and the stars aligned beautifully for your creation. I couldn't wait to meet you.

Being your mother has been a whirlwind, the most incredible thing I've ever done. You've taught me so much. The moment I found out I was going to be a mother for the first time with you, Leudica, there were a lot of mixed emotions: joy, excitement, fear. Close friends and family shared their opinions and advice on being a new mother, but nothing prepares you for it until it happens!

I became a mother early on in our business, and caring for you taught me to be productive and get things done in a meaningful, purposeful way. What I can achieve in a day now compared with 10 years ago is completely different. It takes a village to raise a child, and learning to lean on loved ones has been one of my most liberating lessons.

But what amazed me the most, Leudica, was that I felt connected to you straight away, almost spiritually. The birth didn't go to plan. You were born suddenly and as a C-section. It gave me insight into the next 10 years of being a mother to you and your siblings: that it's not always going to go by the book, and that's ok. For example, sometimes when I'm trying to dress Wolfie and all he wants to do is chat, it reminds me that you all have your own little timetables, your own perspectives and desires, and you've given me permission to be wholly present with you.

My favourite moments with you are the most random ones: the mornings when you all jump into bed with us for cuddles; when we're in the car together and you tell me what's important in your little worlds. Missy, you are the best mother to Wolfie. You show me how to be patient with him. Your love for him is beautiful.

I love to watch you all experience things for the first time that excite you; watch you interact with your friends, showing how much you care for people and how they view the world. Your curiosity about my work gives me confidence, and your curiosity about the world inspires me daily. I love nothing more than coming home to you all.

But I won't lie, there have been tough moments! That's life, after all. Wolfie, learning to be a good mother to a strong, determined young man definitely challenged me and made me grow. It was always hard to go to work and leave you all when you didn't want me to (and when

I didn't want to leave you) and to help you understand that Mummy will always come home to you. I felt a lot of guilt in those first six months, Leudica and Missy, running off to work while other mums could stick around in the schoolyard. But going to work, being inspired and working hard with my team, then coming back to you empowered me. I'm grateful to you guys for helping me learn that.

My childhood was very different from yours. My mother passed away when I was 11, and my time with you makes me cherish the moments I didn't have with my mum. It made me appreciate all these moments so very much more and made me want to instil that love and presence into every moment with you that I could. When we were growing up, my father (your Grandpa) was running a law firm and being a single parent, and he raised us strictly. But your father was raised much more freely. Needless to say, we had two very different approaches to parenting! We've overcome various challenges – I've loosened up and your father's become firmer – but through raising you, we've come to understand each other in deep, beautiful ways we otherwise might not have.

I want you to have an adventurous, fun, culture-rich future that allows you to learn and have different worldly experiences. I want you to be aware of what is going on around you. You know how much I love to travel and taking you all on adventures with us. Seeing the world through your eyes as you soak up different cultures is one of the most beautiful things to behold. You allow us to appreciate things we at times take for granted.

This world is a crazy place, my loves, and I hope you are always safe and happy. But live with your eyes open. I want you to be healthy and have beautiful, meaningful relationships. As you continue to grow and love and evolve, you'll have happiness and disappointment, love and heartbreak, ups and downs. Life's not always fair, but you have the strength and resilience to see you through.

Live your life with pride in your actions and strength in your decisions. Understand your morals and ethics, and check in with them often. If you have dreams, you can do anything you want; just focus. Know your worth and how incredibly precious you are. Great values, amazing friends, incredible family and a beautiful life are all you'll ever need. The world is at your feet and I will always be here behind you.

Love, Mum

> *"Live your life with PRIDE in your actions and STRENGTH in your decisions. Understand your MORALS and ethics, and CHECK IN with them often."*

CANDICE LAKE

PHOTOGRAPHER, BLOGGER, DESIGNER
and CONTRIBUTING STYLE EDITOR at VOGUE AUSTRALIA
Mother to ARDEN and OLYMPIA

While studying law, this London-based Australian was discovered by an Italian modelling agent at the age of 20 and promptly moved to Milan. At the peak of her career, shooting campaigns for Ralph Lauren and Versace with the likes of Bruce Weber, Mario Testino and Steven Meisel, Candice decided to shift her focus and pursue a career behind the lens. She returned briefly to Australia and gained a Bachelor of Fine Art degree, with her graduate show featuring in Vogue. *She has evolved into one of the fashion industry's leading influencers, regularly shooting for Jimmy Choo, Swarovski, Louis Vuitton and Cartier both behind and in front of the lens.*

Now, Candice is undertaking her greatest passion project – juggling motherhood while running her own company. She lives in London near Hampstead Heath, with her husband, architect Didier Ryan, and their two children.
"Motherhood is the most intense relationship I've ever been in – with fierce and endless amounts of love, joy, challenges and accepting the selflessness," she says. "Although more than that, I am constantly trying to see my children for exactly who they are and embracing this. I hope that through unconditional love and spending meaningful time together, they have the self-confidence to be the very best versions of themselves."

"The greatest GIFT
I hope to give you
is not material
possessions, but the
EXPERIENCE of
travelling the world,
wholly and fully,
with your eyes and
HEART wide open."

Darling Arden and Olympia,

This is as much a letter to me as it is to you – a reminder of sorts, to step back and let you find your own path. You came into this life through me, not from me, and I will always be grateful for the honour.

My dreams and hopes for you? That we don't push our own dreams and hopes onto you, but help guide you through life by the example of how we live our lives, so you may follow your own dreams, whatever they may be.

Instead, what I would like to do is to tell you some of the interesting lessons I have learnt (sometimes the hard way) along the way.

The greatest gift I hope to give you is not material possessions, but the experience of travelling the world, wholly and fully, with your eyes and heart wide open.

On your journey through this long life, be sure to walk down the unsigned path. Be not afraid of going the wrong way, going it alone or leaving a place you don't feel is quite right. Fear will only lead to stagnation, and your life should flow like a river.

Work hard doing something you love. Don't be lured by the material; at the end of the day, it is just stuff and I know too many people who appear to have it all and yet are desperately empty. Stuff is just stuff, and if acquiring it is not fun or rewarding, you will never be fulfilled.

Don't take no for an answer – ever. If you really want something, fight for it, even if that means hearing 'no' 30 times. My own mother taught me that.

Natural merit and talent are gifts, of which you both have bountiful amounts; but never rely on just these. Strive to be the very best at whatever it is you love to do. If you put in the effort, your rewards will be plentiful.

Grab every opportunity in front of you. Be kind and grateful, and never forget where these opportunities came from. Life is a lottery, so work hard, but never forget how lucky you are to have been born into the world as you have.

Always hold the door open for someone and wave at the driver of the car who lets you in front of them.

Always look someone in the eye when you are speaking to them. And never look at your phone when you're speaking with someone or when you're at the table – it's desperately rude.

Don't gossip – it implies you have nothing of value to add – and never exaggerate. You're interesting enough, so you don't need to do that. Be punctual – because being late essentially is telling someone you think your time is more important than theirs; it is not.

Be a kind person. Always ask yourself how you would feel if someone did that to you. But have no regrets; every mistake you make is an opportunity to improve yourself. If you don't make mistakes, you're not trying hard enough.

Soak up knowledge from everywhere. Learn as much as you can from as many sources; you can never know enough about anything. Open your eyes.

Enjoy the small moments in your life – all of them. Because when you break it down, the essence of your life is how much you enjoy the moments in between. If you're waiting around for something big, you will miss all the truly special times.

One dream I do have is that you forever stay as connected to nature as you are now. That you always walk through forests picking blackberries, finding frogs, identifying trees and mushrooms. That you continue to dance through the bush meeting birds and dragonflies, discovering ladybugs under rocks and getting lost in its magic. I hope you grow old still loving planting seeds and watching them grow, no matter the size of your garden. Being connected to nature is something we have tried passionately to cultivate in you both from birth.

Never look to others to see what they're doing; only look within yourself. If your heart says jump, do so with wild abandon.

Never be afraid to turn left when everyone is going right. Be proud of being different and always think outside the box. Difference is what makes people fascinating.

I fell in love with your father because he was like no one else I had ever met before. I hope you never settle for anything less. Settling is a waste of your life. You only get one shot, so don't blow it by walking with someone who is 'almost good enough'. Love passionately, but never lean on that person to carry you. Only you can carry yourself.

Be humble like your father. Take risks and don't ever be afraid to question authority – authority must be earned. Question everything.

And after all this, shall I tell you the ultimate secret? It is curiosity. Curiosity is the fountain of youth. Never, ever stop being curious. When your curiosity dies, so, too, does your spirit.

I love you both more than I ever knew possible. You have been the greatest gifts life has ever presented me, and I am eternally grateful for every small moment I get to walk beside you.

Love, Mummy

AMBRE DAHAN

FOUNDER OF SPRWMN and AMBRE VICTORIA JEWELRY
Mother to ELLA and BILLIE

Ambre Dahan grew up in Paris (which would explain why she's so effortlessly
chic) and now lives in Los Angeles with her two daughters. She's the founder
of contemporary clothing brand SPRWMN (pronounced 'Superwoman'),
a line of leather and suede basics handmade entirely from French hides. She's
also the founder of Ambre Victoria Jewelry, which is all handmade in LA.
"I was always overdressed at school, which raised some teachers' eyebrows."

One of the many endearing things about Ambre is her honesty. "When I separated
from my ex-husband, Billie was only two and a half. I felt a huge responsibility to
make their life amazing and for them never to feel like they were not growing up in
a happy family. I had to be stronger than ever and I really think I succeeded.
My girls and I have an amazing relationship," she says.

Dear Ella and Billie,

I grew up in Paris and travelled all over the world with my parents. It was an urban, bohemian and worldly childhood. We spent our summers in Ibiza and I feel very fortunate that my parents allowed us to experience so much. Even all the crazy bumps in the road made us fit for everything in life.

I remember being exposed to a lot of beautiful things, but I think that you don't realise the environment you live in until you grow up, start travelling, leave home and have time to reflect.

I try to fill our lives with lots of things – fun, creativity, excitement, adventure, as well as responsibility and kindness. For me, life in LA is paradise, and I hope you feel the same! It's the perfect mix of everything – nature, ocean, space and city. It took me time to create that environment and I'm very grateful for our LA family.

I try to be a very present mother. I take you everywhere with me. And while I am far from being perfect, we have a lot of fun and there is a lot of craziness happening. We have a very honest relationship.

I run two fashion businesses and I hope you've seen how important it is to work hard and that things don't come easily. I've always loved fashion. When I was growing up, your grandmother loved Azzedine Alaïa and I remember going to his little shop as a kid. I also remember the over-the-knee boots your grandfather bought me from Jean Paul Gaultier when I was 14.

You are exposed to amazing people on a daily basis. You both see me work hard and I always share my ideas with you when I get inspired. You'll often come to my office or my photo shoots.

At times, it has been challenging being a single mother and raising you on my own, but we are so close and definitely have the most amazing bond. But doing it alone can be hard. Sometimes, I still want to cry or stay in bed; but life goes on and I am a very positive person.

I'll always be honest with you and teach you that life is not easy – you need to know that from a young age. At school, be yourselves and have confidence. We are living in a scary world; the rules have changed and social media is not helping. I hope I can always teach you to be both strong and kind.

Love, Mom

SHEN-TEL LEE

ENTREPRENEUR / Mother to BENJAMIN and KINGSTON

Shen-Tel Lee has a long list of accomplishments, but her proudest by far are her two boys, Benjamin and Kingston. After enduring a gruelling three-year struggle to conceive, Shen-Tel turned to IVF, with successful results. But the process wasn't without its challenges. "I now speak openly about infertility. I still think there is a huge stigma about it in our society today and that people are not informed enough about how common it is," she explains. "I sometimes think we, as women, have got it all wrong... We are told our careers are everything and that we can have children later in life. This isn't the case for everyone and I feel like we should encourage women to have kids younger and to know more about what our fertility is from a younger age."

Sydney-born Shen-Tel moved to Malaysia after marrying her high-school sweetheart, Bobby Ting, and it's there her two thriving businesses are based – the accessories brand Sereni & Shentel and jewellery brand Bowerhaus. She credits her mother, Dame Betty Lee, for giving her the confidence to chase her dreams: "The greatest gift she gave me was that she instilled in me a confidence that I can do anything, and it is something I hope to instil in my boys." The family returned recently to Shen-Tel's hometown of Sydney for the boys' schooling.

Dearest Benjamin and Kingston,

Gosh, you both are such a good time. The days are tediously long, but you grow up so fast! Don't be disheartened when, at times, our opinions inadvertently clash; it's only because Mummy wishes to instil impeccable manners so you both grow up to be law-abiding citizens. I want everyone who gets to know either of you to say, "Gosh, I want to meet the remarkable parents who raised such a charming and caring gentleman."

The minute each of you were born, I cried tears of joy. Motherhood made me realise the sacrifices and struggles my parents went through to raise me. I not only became a more respectful and appreciative daughter, but a much better human being at multitasking. I pray that both of you will experience the delight of fatherhood, as only then will you fully appreciate the depth of my insane and unconditional, militant love.

Prior to your arrivals, I had no idea how much my life was going to change. Suddenly the definition of hard work included wrangling you both off to school with the much dreaded 'strict government-regulated' packed lunches that do not contain nuts or eggs, lest you endanger the wellbeing of one of your anaphylactic schoolmates. Modern parenthood sure comes with an ever-changing list of weird and strange demands.

The List so far:

Keep out of jail.

Don't kill your classmates with food!

I know it was a traumatic time when we moved you away from your comfortable lives in Borneo and relocated to Sydney. There were months of readjustments, when you both missed the opulence of the home you grew up in – one with drivers, bodyguards and nannies. We wanted to provide you both with the skills and tools to be able to fend for yourselves, to be your own person, and not live your life bathing in the glory of your high-profile family name back in Asia.

For us, your independence is the most important gift we can give you, and that the move to Sydney while both of you were very young would give you both the best start in life. As your parents, we could not be more pleased to have made the transition, as we truly believe this is for your own good. Your Kuching home will always be there – a place you can always return to when you're older, if you choose to.

Remember when you both asked me where babies come from? I looked at your dad and laughed. I have never shared with you the book that my parents read to me, *Where did I Come From?*. That's because it doesn't actually cover your conception.

Back in the early 1980s, IVF technology was still in its infancy. Today, this kind of expertise is prevalent. Yes, both of you are IVF babies; scientific miracles that took me on a rather extraordinary journey to motherhood. An odyssey that both your dad and I happily chose to take, because we wanted you so much. It wasn't easy at times, and the struggle to fall pregnant had emotional and disruptive ramifications, not only on me, but on your father and grandparents, as well. Life lessons taught me that we are not dealt the same cards and that, when things get difficult, it is the love and support of caring family members and loyal friends that pull us through trying times. Never take them for granted.

The List so far:

Keep out of jail.

Don't kill your classmates with food!

Keep your family close.

It seems like it is so much harder to be parents nowadays. Back when I was growing up, it was acceptable to be smacked when we did something wrong. We actually feared our parents, because it was a generation who subscribed to the notion of 'spare the rod and spoil the child'. My mum just had to flash me the 'look' and I knew instantly I was in trouble. In fact,

we were told that if our parents didn't smack us it meant they didn't care about us. Such parental 'privilege' is no longer legally or socially acceptable, but I can tell you that my generation all listened and obeyed our parents unquestioningly. It's so laughable how times have changed: your punishments now consist of the 'naughty corner' and disconnecting your WiFi.

Let's talk about the time when I completely lost it. When I first moved to Kuching from Sydney after I married your father, I lost my identity; I was only ever known as the daughter-in-law of a prominent family. It disturbed me, because I knew I was much more than that. It fuelled a fire in me to re-establish myself and prove that I was still the same happy, liberated and independent individual.

I chose to maintain my maiden name, because I wanted you both to know that being married and being a mum doesn't define me. Always remember, you never need to change who you are for someone else. You must always know your own worth and never compromise your principles. It's these qualities that can best define you.

Benjamin, you know how you constantly get upset because Kingston has a habit of intuitively annoying the crap out of you? I know this feeling of uncontrollable rage. There was a time when I was so angry and sad; it lasted for weeks. I didn't know it then, but I was suffering from post-natal depression. Again, my sense of identity had been compromised, or so I thought. In actual fact, I had just added a few more hurdles to the track.

For you, I liken it to the feeling you got when I didn't buy you that Kinder Surprise egg at the supermarket. There were tears, anger and rage. It was not fun and no one really likes to talk about it, because being sad is, well, really wretchedly miserable. Thankfully, now I know there is always a reason for sadness and it's best to talk about it to someone rather than bottling it up inside. I will always be here for you, no matter how old you are or how old I am. Please pick up the phone and call me. I love a chat.

One crucial piece of advice is to think twice before you contemplate doing anything reckless. The digital world can be most unforgiving, and retributions are swift, brutal and merciless. I wish I could erase certain objectionable articles from the internet, but sadly, I can't. I'm afraid the day will come when you are both old enough to Google the chronological history of your forefathers' past, which was often unjustly portrayed. I hope both of you take pride in their accomplishments, and please be gentle with their shortcomings. There are lessons to be learnt from their hindsight.

Both sets of grandparents love both of you very much and are almost too generous to a fault. You must remember that we would not be here without them. Maybe it's time to read *Where Did I Come From?*...

All I want for you both is to find your true calling in life. I knew from a young age that I was a creative person. However, it took me years of hard and confronting challenges to realise that my place in this world is to design. I was pleased that I remain true to my passion, because nothing beats being happy doing something I enjoy.

I want you to keep trying new things, no matter how difficult they are – the only way to know what you love is to get up and do it. When you figure it out, my only advice is to keep running in that direction (jump the hurdles); don't listen to the naysayers. Follow your gut and you both will go far. Be what you wish to be and live your own dream. I am so lucky to have you.

The List

Keep out of jail.

Don't kill your classmates with food!

Keep your family close.

Live your own dream.

... and don't forget to brush your teeth. Oral hygiene is most important.

Lovingly yours forever, Mum

DEBBIE TAN

Co-owner of AQUABUMPS / Mother to JET and SPIKE

For former advertising manager Debbie Tan, motherhood was the catalyst for a career change. After her sons arrived, the dynamic mother left behind her magazine career and turned her focus to her photographer husband Eugene Tan's business Aquabumps, an iconic Australian website and daily email newsletter dedicated to beach life.

They're the dream team – Debbie heads up the commercial side of their thriving business, while Eugene runs the creative arm. Their life is based around Sydney's iconic Bondi Beach, and it's here, when she's not working or with her boys, that she loves to unwind with a run and swim.

Dearest Jet and Spike,

I strive to be a strong, loving and independent mother. My mum – your grandmother – had me as a single mum and brought me into the world on her own, giving birth to me in the dorm room of the hotel she worked at in New Zealand.

I didn't realise the magnitude of that until I became a mother myself. The inner strength she must have had to have endured that on her own. She gave me up for adoption the next day and went back to work.

One month later, she changed her mind and came back for me. She hadn't even told her family that she'd given birth to a child – it was 43 years ago now. So she wrote a telegram to her sister, brought me home from New Zealand to Australia and, for those first few years, I was brought up by my mum, my Nana, who called me Pixie, and her sister, Lesley.

On reflection and in retrospect, it made me the woman and mother I am today – to love, to live from my heart and to show my boys that women are independent and strong, and we can do whatever we put our hearts and minds to as long as it comes from a place of love. Just like my mum did for me.

My parents were very relaxed and open with me as a child. They didn't have much money, but what they didn't have, they made up for with time and dedication to us kids.

They gave me my first alcoholic drink and cigarette, to scare me more than anything, I think. It kind of worked, because when the kids at school asked me behind the shed for a ciggie, I'd reply, "Nah, I've tried it. It's gross."

Their style is ingrained in me, but I still do it my way. It's different raising you in the city – I grew up in the country with so much freedom and space. We live in a beachside city suburb, so giving you freedom is harder, as there are more dangers and roads to cross, and things that can go wrong.

I hope you'll always cherish the time we spend at our little house up the coast, where we've tried to give you a bit more freedom. It feels like home there and is my favourite place in the world.

I told your dad after a few catch-ups – not really even proper dates – that we were going to be together forever. He looked at me blankly like I was crazy, but here we are, 12 years on.

I found out I was pregnant three days before I married your dad. I called him and he was driving, and all I could hear was cheering in the distance. I later found out he was hanging out of his van, beeping and cheering with joy.

I want you to live a happy life; a contented, full life. I want freedom and choice and health for you. I want you to be open and to love without holding back; to know that you can choose to do whatever you want in your lives knowing we will support you every step of the way.

I want you to know that when it comes to achieving your dreams, anything is possible. Look at your dad, boys. He quit his day job to follow his dreams of starting Aquabumps. I left a small country town to come to the big smoke in the hope of working in an advertising agency.

> "You are my everything, my BEATING HEART. I never knew I could love something or someone as much as I LOVE YOU."

We are your perfect role models for knowing that whatever you dream is possible. Your dad and I both encourage you to follow what makes your hearts sing and, as much as we would love you to take over the family business, it's all up to you.

To me, success means accomplishing something you put your heart into. To try your best; to have fun while you are in it. It's *being*, not always working towards something! Ultimately, it's about giving it your all. And that doesn't have to mean coming first or being the best, but knowing that you have dug deep and given it your best shot.

Your dad and I have tried to educate you about 'experiences' over 'things'. You'll get so much more lasting joy from being somewhere new, learning about a culture, an experience. I will keep encouraging this and showing you the simple beauty in the sunrise, the light, the sunset.

I've learnt that the greatest gifts in life come with age – you gather more experiences, you celebrate milestones with the ones you love, you accept what you have been given and you realise what's really important. So I welcome getting older with the people I love – with you both, with your dad, with my friends and family.

You are my everything, my beating heart. I never knew I could love something or someone as much as I love you. You've taught me to go slow, to stop and smell the roses, to be in the moment and to find joy in the little things. Creating you is my greatest achievement and my most treasured gift, my meaning of all that is love.

Love, Mum

HELENA VESTERGAARD

Helena Vestergaard launched full-tilt into her role as mum to baby River (now one year old) with fresh eyes and a fresh spirit, and, as she admits, a certain naivety. "I had no idea what it was going to be like having a baby, let alone a newborn! I didn't even know that babies woke up during the night. But the love that you have for your baby gets you through it."

Helena and her pro-surfer partner, Nathan Webster, lead an idyllic life filled with sun, sand and waves on Sydney's Northern Beaches. When they're not swimming at their local beaches, rock pools or lagoons, they can be found happily at home, eating healthy food and taking on the shared and committed responsibility of looking after River.

Dear River,

I have always dreamt of being a mother, of playing with you, making your meals, talking to you about your day and just loving you to pieces. In the beginning, when you first arrived, you were very sick and I had so much anxiety. I really struggled. I also had no idea what to expect from a newborn. I actually didn't know a thing about babies!

After many months of sleepless nights, anxiety attacks and an almost total meltdown, I finally caved in and had a baby guru come to teach me how to put you on a routine. It was the best thing I ever did and I am so lucky to have your dad, who is so supportive and helpful. One day, if you have children of your own, you'll discover that mothers are so hard on themselves. Always ask for help when you need it.

You are such a happy little thing. You will always give me a smile – the cheekiest smile in the world – and you have the cutest little voice I've ever heard. You're so independent, but you love interacting with people, too. I don't know where you've got it from, as both your dad and I are quite introverted.

I can't believe you are one already! You've grown so fast and, while each milestone is so exciting, I also want you to be my little baby forever.

Being a mother, I feel I have found my true purpose. This idea truly has got me through some incredibly tough times, as has the support of your dad and my family. The love I feel for you is euphoric and I couldn't imagine life without you. Motherhood has completely changed my life for the better.

I want you to know I will always be there for you, no matter what. I'll always be here to give you advice and help you navigate life's ups and downs.

When it comes to relationships, something I want you to understand is that the way people behave says far more about them than it does about you. But it is also important to know your values and respect yourself enough to speak up when it is necessary.

Always know your worth. You deserve the world, so don't settle for anything less. And slow down and be in the moment – this is something you will learn with age.

Criticism is always hard, and rejection can be the toughest feeling, but also the greatest teacher. I don't want you to see failure as the end of the world; rather, a stepping-stone to something better. For me, the fear of failure has stopped me from trying many things in life, which is sad, because we all judge ourselves so harshly.

I will show you that there is actually no such thing as failure; it's just judgement that you put on yourself. Try everything, and if you are better or worse at some things, so what?! That's what makes us all unique.

Success to me is health and happiness. The idea that you have to work yourself to the bone to be successful is not something I believe in. I believe the meaning of success is to be content within yourself. At the end of the day, what success is to you will not always be the same for someone else. We all have to choose our own values. I want you to work hard at something you are passionate about, so you can enjoy the things that are important to you.

The abuse of the planet is something I worry about, and I wish we could do more to protect nature for you.

Also, you are having to navigate social media and the sexualised and unequal world we currently live in. I want you to know that women are powerful and deserve a seat at the table. I want you to know that your choices have repercussions, so think of the planet and its future in all that you do, as the smallest things can help.

And I will forever be grateful you chose me to be your mother.

Love, Mama

> "*The LOVE I feel for you is EUPHORIC and I couldn't imagine life without YOU. Motherhood has completely CHANGED my life for the BETTER.*"

LIA-BELLE KING

CO-FOUNDER of WORN STORE / Mother to OPHELIA

It was after working in their respective industries for more than a decade that Lia-Belle King and her wife, Lotte Barnes, decided to take a few months off and travel to Bali, India, Nepal and Sri Lanka. Within two weeks of leaving Australia, they had decided not to go back, a move that was to lead them to their next calling in life.

Living in Bali and sourcing furniture for their villa, the couple discovered a talented local artisan whom they worked with to have a chair made. Lia-Belle posted an image of the chair on her Instagram account and, overnight, people were posting requests to buy one. And so, with a single 'Sling' chair, the furniture and lifestyle brand Worn was born. The couple has since returned to Australia and, in seeking a slower life, now live with their daughter, Ophelia, in a beautiful 1900s former principal's cottage, situated on nine hectares of bushland in the Byron Bay hinterland.

My darling Ophelia,

A note to myself, to other mothers and, of course, to you.

My wife takes out the garbage and pumps the water up from the creek. She puts on her rubber boots and opens the gate for the chickens to roam; cuts back the overly enthusiastic jasmine that threatens to drown the handrail on the verandah. She does the big jobs, the dirty jobs; the ones I'd prefer not to. She does them as a gesture of love, but also because someone has to.

I do the details – the daily sideshows of role-play with Dolly, where together we get dressed and eat our lunch and change our nappy and, look how much fun we're having. The endless loads of washing and strategically planned grocery trips. The details – like timing my two glasses of wine with your next feed. Like not taking pain relief even when I need it. The details – like knowing broccoli was last week and this week it's all about peas. It's the hours spent researching 3.5-tog sleep suits, drawing the lavender baths, no fruit after three, music class on Tuesdays and swimming class on Fridays that keep it all together.

Before you were born, your mama changed the way I experienced the world. She undressed me from my Dries Van Noten pantsuit, removed my almond-toed heels and cracked my chest open so widely it finally created enough space for my heart to swell. She let the sunshine in. Two years together and swollen with love for her and, for the first time, myself, it was only natural that expansion would soon grow to include a baby.

Three moon cycles of me searching blindly for you in my sleep. Pleading, praying, negotiating with my father to find you in that other-side place and bring you to me.

Eventually... two pink lines.

During the pregnancy, I was exhausted, restless and delighted. It would be my one-and-only opportunity to carry a child, and those 10 months were the closest I will ever come to enlightenment.

A week before your birth – a flood. A good omen. Two days before your birth, a snake appeared above the doorway of our house – a python, tangled around the eaves, its tail hanging languidly. Another good omen. The birth. You came in such a hurry and I didn't make a sound.

For the first year of your life, I kept a running timeline of where my life would be had I *not* had you. I watched my friends and thought about how my career would have evolved, where I would have been living, travelling.

Then your first birthday arrived and those images dissolved. The maiden flew the roost and now a mother stood, proud and devoted.

The new me swallowed the old me. Down with a swig of apple cider vinegar went the vanity, the selfishness, the ambition and most of the moodiness. What once defined me was no longer relevant. I had been holding on to an outdated version of myself and couldn't give in to personal growth without surrendering to motherhood entirely.

So I did, I did the full surrender, 'mum jeans' and all.

I am not the mother I thought I would be. Sometimes I am stronger, more graceful, more complex and less patient. I'm not as holistic as I thought I would be, either, but I'm softer and much quieter. I realise and accept that the model of motherhood I had imagined for myself was loosely based on my own childhood experience. While I crave a successful career beyond motherhood that my own mother did not, it doesn't mean I am any less fulfilled by my role.

My daughter, should you read this one day (and I will ensure that you do), you are and will always be, the only and greatest love I will ever bear from my own body.

If I'm honest with myself, and with you, putting my career on hold has, at times, been crippling to my self-esteem. But despite my own needs both personally and professionally, you are my first priority and there could never be anything more urgent, more demanding, more essential or more required than the meeting of your needs and the delivery of your happiness. Despite my love for myself, my love for you is infinitely greater.

Know that your pain is my pain, and I fear all the times you'll learn something painful about the world.

Grow to know that if you don't agree with something, you can and should speak up. Even to me. Know that your differences are your strengths and your educated voice is important and valued. Know that, at times, I will be hard. Hard to be with, hard on you and hard on myself.

Watch me continue to try becoming the best I can for you. I know I will falter; even knowing that, and that you'll see it, makes me feel unworthy. But please know that when I do, I will ask to try again and again. And again.

Love, your Mummy

> *"There could NEVER be anything more ESSENTIAL... than the delivery of your HAPPINESS."*

VANESSA BREUER

MODEL / Mother to LUCA and EVIE

Vanessa Breuer's modelling works takes her around the globe, but when she's back in her adopted home of Ibiza, her life is all about precious family time and making memories her two children will treasure forever.

Growing up in Germany, Breuer was discovered when she was 14 years old, while working as a cleaner at a florist. She moved to London and then to New York, before landing in Sydney, where she met Oddy, the man who would later become her husband. Having lived and worked in busy cities for years and craving the slow life, the former Victoria's Secret model and certified therapeutic chef moved with Oddy and their five-month-old daugher, Luca, to a 250-year-old farmhouse on Ibiza. It was there, in their hilltop home, that their second child, Evie, was born.

Dear Luca and Evie,

I don't know if words can ever describe the bond a mother feels with her children. It's a feeling of oneness. You are part of me and I am part of you. The love for you runs through my veins and is something that can never be taken away.

Life is all about love – it's security, warmth, comfort. It's the energy that surrounds us. The spark between us, the connection; the sparkle in the eye, the soft touch that keeps you in this world. At the end of the day, we don't need much. Love is the most important thing.

I was raised by strict parents in Germany. We had a lot of structure and order in our life. My father left when I was four; he wasn't a big influence in my life. Your grandmother fell mentally ill when I was about nine, and she spent a lot of time in hospital. I'd stay with other families or friends for weeks and months at a time.

She raised me to be super-independent (especially from men, which was important to her). She always trusted me and believed I was capable of figuring things out myself.

Although I had a lot of anger and sadness growing up, it made me who I am today, so I have her to be thankful to for raising me this way. There was never a lack of love and I truly believe she tried the best she could, but due to her illness it was hard at times.

I was scouted by a model agent at the age of 14 while I was working as a cleaner at the local florist. I moved to London at the age of 15, then New York at 16, and modelled all over the world.

I met your dad, Oddy, when I moved to Australia. Before I met him, I wasn't sure about having children, but that all changed when I fell deeply in love with your dad. When I fell pregnant, I took a break from modelling and did something I had always wanted to do – a course at a culinary school in Berkeley, California, which inspired me to focus on eating local, seasonal produce and cooking mostly at home.

Now, Ibiza is our home. I still remember meeting your dad here for a holiday when we were still in a long-distance relationship. I came from New York and he came from Sydney – we hadn't seen each other for about three months. It felt like all our worries disappeared when we arrived, and we fell in love with each other all over again. Ibiza had the right energy for us.

Years later, we got married on the island. It always held a special place in our hearts and it felt like the right place to start life in Europe, the slower life we craved. At first, we planned to stay for one year and move on, but we're still here after four. Evie, you were born at home here.

They say the island chooses you, and it really welcomed us with open arms. We live a totally different life from what we've ever lived before. We'd always moved from one crazy, busy city to the next, but when we got here we craved the opposite, so we live in isolation surrounded by nature on top of a hill.

We live in a 250-year-old farmhouse and love it. There are times when I miss my chic New York apartment, but we enjoy the challenges and they keep us busy. Life here is all about you, our girls.

Luca, you tell me, "Mama, I love you infinity." I hope you will always say that, as it makes my heart melt. You also say "broccodi", which I much prefer to the actual word.

Evie, you walk around giggling to yourself and I hope you never lose your free, loving spirit. You both make me enjoy the little things in life – the simplicity. My eyes sparkle thinking of you both.

I'll always be here for you. I'll always listen to you. I hope I can teach you to be honest and proud of yourselves. I want you to live a life in peace, surrounded by the things that matter – family, love, nature. I want you to be kids for as long as possible. Life is full of things we should and shouldn't be doing: responsibilities. I want you to enjoy the 'bliss bubble' you have being kids. I don't want you to worry. I want you always to be yourselves and I don't want you ever to stop asking questions. There is so much to learn. Always.

You've shown me infinite love. You've made me who I am right now and I am happy to be in this place. My world will forever be changed, because I will always be connected to you, no matter what happens.

Love, Mama

> *"I want you to live a life in PEACE, surrounded by the things that matter – FAMILY, LOVE, NATURE. I want you to BE KIDS for as long as possible."*

ELIF SHAFAK

AUTHOR / Mother to ZELDA and ZAHIR

"Motherhood has taught me the gift of love, the joy of learning and the humble acceptance that we are, no matter what our age, essentially students of life," says the internationally bestselling Turkish author.

Elif Shafak was raised by two women, her single mother – a secular diplomat – and her traditional grandmother, who nurtured her love of storytelling. She has written 16 books (translated into 48 languages), including *The Bastard of Istanbul* and *Black Milk*, an intimate memoir exploring motherhood, creativity, writing and her own struggle with postnatal depression.

"I love connecting with lives beyond my own little, limited life – reaching out to minds and hearts," she says. "That feeling of timelessness, placelessness, as though words were the magic carpets carrying us to lands afar. You write for weeks and months and years on your own, hunched at your desk, not knowing who will read this story and whether it will mean anything to anyone. You keep the faith and carry on and then, one day, long after, a reader sends a letter or comes to a book signing, dragging along their friends and whole family, and says, 'You know I read your book and you have no idea what it meant to me.'"

Dear Zelda and Zahir,

At the ages of one and three, you have both moved from Istanbul to London with me. You have learnt quickly about airports, train stations, national borders, passport controls... And as time went by, you also learnt that, thankfully, there are many things in life that can travel across borders in need of no visas: ideas, stories, music, food, love, laughter. These belong to all humanity equally, regardless of race, gender, nationality.

Zahir, when you were at nursery school, your teacher asked the children what mothers did. Many mentioned things like, "They bake cakes, they make nice food, they walk in the park, they take the dog to the vet, they work in the office, they invite guests over..." You shook your head. Your answer was, "Mothers listen to loud heavy-metal music – boom, boom, boom – while they write books."!

Zelda, when you were in primary school, a student said that people in Africa and the Middle East were backward. You got very upset. "They are not backward," you said. "You just haven't heard their stories yet."

There is no 'us' and there is no 'them'. There are people whose stories we are famliar with and people whose stories we have not heard yet. This I learnt from you both. It is amazing to see how much motherhood has taught and how deeply it has changed and moulded me; softened my corners, turned me into a different and, hopefully, better person. I was scared, at first, that I might find it all hard to juggle, and there were moments when it felt it was. But out of the challenges came beauty and balance. Until you were born, Zelda, I had lived the life of a nomad.

Here is my background: Born in Strasbourg, France, I was raised in Ankara, Turkey, by a single working mother and a spiritual grandmother. After my parents got divorced, my mum brought me to my grandma's house. Mum was only 19 years old when she got married – imagine. She had dropped out of school, despite her mother's objections, and followed my father to France, deeply in love.

When the marriage collapsed and my mother returned to Turkey, she therefore had no diploma, no money, nowhere else to go. The neighbours instantly began looking for a suitable husband for my mother, in part because a young divorcee was regarded as a danger to the whole community. It was my grandma who stopped them. She said, "My daughter should graduate, have a career; she should have choices in life. She can always get married again, if she wants to."

Grandma raised me while my mother went back to university, graduating with flying colours and becoming first a teacher, then a successful diplomat. The solidarity between my uneducated, Eastern grandmother and well-educated, Westernised mother left a big impact on me, showing me how crucial it was for women to have networks of support and sisterhood. It also made me more aware of gender bias and gender discrimination, having grown up observing the hardships that my mother had to go through in a patriarchal culture such as Turkey was back then – and still is today.

Until I started college, I had seen my father only twice, brief encounters where he didn't say or ask much. I met my half-brothers only in my mid-20s. Coming from a dysfunctional family affected me and my writing in many ways. Feeling like an 'insider-outsider' in my motherland, I have always felt close to the 'other'.

I've lived in many places over time – Madrid, Amman, Cologne, Boston, Michigan, Arizona – and in-between, always, always Istanbul, the city I have loved passionately and whose stories I continue to tell. Then, London, with its precious diversity – the city of traditions old and dreams new. So, life has always been peripatetic.

When asked where home is, my first inclination has always been to ask a question back: "*Homes*, if you will. Can we not have multiple homes?"

Writing is not a job; it is not a career. Nor is it a hobby. It is how you breathe, who you are, your skin and flesh and soul. When you devote your life to books and stories, writing becomes your life. And the world of a writer is a self-centred one, based on solitude. Novelists are lonely creatures, often with inflated egos. I was worried I might not be able to balance the introverted energy of writing with the selfless giving of motherhood. I had all these concerns and more. How utterly silly I was, back then.

Of course, motherhood changed me, and it changed me completely, radically, and in so many wonderful and unexpected ways that I have only gratitude in my heart. It has not been an easy journey, sometimes. There were bumps and struggles along the way, and that's very normal. We need to understand that, like everything else in life, motherhood has its ups and downs. We need to allow women and children to talk about those, too.

The over-romanticised, over-polished myth of motherhood is not helping anyone. We need honest conversations about what it means to be a mother, a parent, a daughter or a son, and how similar we are across the world; how fragile and how strong, how complex and simply human.

And you two, with your distinct personalities, have taught me that love grows bigger the more you share, and that generosity of spirit is contagious – we learn it from each other. For the path you have opened to this clumsy traveller, I am immensely grateful to you both, my children.

Your Mother

BRIDGET YORSTON

CO-FOUNDER *of fashion label BEC + BRIDGE*
Mother to TOMMY, GEORGE and TILLY

As a mother of three and co-director of a flourishing Australian fashion label
– which marked its 15th year in business in 2017, has two standalone retail
stores and celebrity fans including Rhianna, Kim Kardashian and Miranda
Kerr – Sydney-based Bridget Yorston has her hands full.
But she wouldn't have it any other way. "I truly believe that becoming
a mother allowed me to look at my brand with fresh eyes," she says.

"Of course there have been many challenges, too… Starting with the initial adjustments
of going back to work and having to leave my babies, to having to accept that I no longer
have the extra hours that I'd like to dedicate to work. And let's not forget the guilt! That
universal mother's guilt where it doesn't matter what you do, you feel guilty."
Luckily, she has an incredibly supportive business partner in Bec Cooper (the pair met
on their first day at uni and became best friends). They both credit their strong
partnership as a defining part of their success and it's also allowed them to both lean
out at different times when they've had newborn babies.
A devout Christan (her husband, Ed Yorston, is a pastor) Bridget lives by the teachings
of Proverbs 22:6: 'Start children off on the way they should go, and even when they
are old they will not turn from it.'

To my absolute favourites,

I love you all so much it hurts. When I creep into your bedrooms to check on you each night, all I want to do is eat your soft cheeks and smother you in kisses, and squeeze every inch of your bodies. You melt me.

As you grow up in the world, you'll often be made to feel that what matters most is what you do, what you have and who you know. I want to tell you that what matters to me, more than any of these things, is *who* you are. What matters to me is your character. I long for you to keep bearing the fruits of God's Spirit: 'love, joy, peace, patience, kindness, goodness, faithfulness, gentleness and self-control' (Galatians 5:22-23). This is what makes me happiest!

Tommy, I love to see your gentleness through the way you look after your little sister. I've loved watching you grow in empathy, the way you're learning to think beyond your own interests and think about the interests of others. I love your silliness and sense of humour, they bring so much joy to my day.

George, your kindness warms my heart. I know that it's genuine, too. It comes from deep in your heart. I also love your spiritual appetite – it pushes me and challenges me daily. God has blessed you with these gifts and I pray that you'll do mighty things with them!

And Tilly-girl, I love your joyful disposition. I love watching you follow your big brothers around, pretending to be a fierce ninja one minute and a dainty ballerina the next, spinning and twirling in your tutu. At the moment, we're working on patience and self-control – albeit tricky characteristics to grasp as a three-year-old... Let's keep pushing through together, my littlest love.

My loves, keep growing and developing your character, and other good things will follow. These characteristics will increase your emotional intelligence. They will give you the ability to live and work peacefully and happily alongside others. Most significantly, they will make you a beautiful person – the kind of person that people want to be around, a person of integrity and passion and truth.

Whatever path God might lead each of you through life, keep leaning into Him. He might help you grow and evolve and develop these characteristics of 'love, joy, peace, patience, kindness, goodness, faithfulness, gentleness and self-control'. If you do, not only will it make me so happy and proud, but I have no doubt you will change the world just as dramatically as you have all changed mine.

I love you forever, Mumma

PS I'll be creeping into your bedrooms at night to smother you in kisses for as long as I can get away with it!

JENNIFER GRANT

ART DIRECTOR and FOUNDER of ROMEO + JULES
Mother to HARRY and OSCAR

Stationery has always been a passion for Jennifer Grant. At the age of six, she told her mother that she would no longer need to attend school, as she would be taking up the profession of "colour-er". And, just in case that didn't work out, she created her own business cards for when she became the first female president of the United States. "It's been said that I've been 'particular' from an early age, but I read that to mean ambitious!" she says.

Fast-forward to an art director role at *GQ* magazine in New York, and then a surprise move to London, where she landed herself the position at British *Vogue*. Two children (and a dog) later, she launched Romeo + Jules, a bespoke stationery range.

"Success means finding a balance between the life and career I've worked so hard to achieve," says Jennifer. "I decided to launch my brand, first and foremost to give me a creative outlet and so I could juggle my time with two young children. And second, to disarm the concept that stationery needs to be formal. I love the idea of sending a card that bears a sweet (or cheeky!) phrase to bring a smile to the receiver's face."

She encourages her boys to be creative, but never forces it upon them. "Thankfully, they both love to colour and paint and create, which warms my heart," she says. "I do wonder at times if the art supplies I purchase are with the children in mind or, not-so-secretly, for me."

List of little loves for my darling Harrison

Your eyes are truly the windows to your soul. They can be shy sometimes, but those hazel-with-a-tint-of-baby-blue beauties express so much emotion for those who hold a special place in your heart.

Your love of green apples knows no end.

Your excitement for a new day can mean early wake-ups, but your enthusiasm is too admirable to ignore.

Your head is forever creating. I often find you mid-thought and wonder what colours you see, what your ideas look like. I envision your brain to be divided straight down the middle – half daydreamer and half engineer. And I so admire your tenacity and how you strive for your own unique vision, in your own time. Except when we are attempting to get ready for school…

You'd happily live life naked.

There are times when I wonder if you were sent to me to be my guiding light, to give me direction, to shape my thoughts. I think you've parented me so much more than I can begin to understand at this moment.

You have the memory of an elephant and remember every detail.

Your arrival as the firstborn made me understand the saying 'The little things are the big things'.

Handsome Harry, my little man through and through, I couldn't adore you more. I am truly in awe as I watch you grow into your old soul, day by day, phase by phase.

I am one lucky Mama.

Love you beyond.

List of little loves for Oscar wild(e)

Oooh, my cheeky, cheeky boy. Where do I begin? You entered this world with a roar that has not quieted one tiny little bit. Your lust for life shines bright, that's for sure.

Those crystal-blue eyes and beach-blond curls will no doubt get you out of some sticky situations in your future. Those, alongside your ability to turn on the charm at the exact moment you can sense the moment turning sour, will lead to some interesting life stories.

You've never met a pancake you didn't like.

You have a heart of gold and a smile to match. I know for sure that your brother takes up quite a lot of real estate in that big heart of yours.

Everything you do is done with such a commanding personality, and you've been this way since very early days. Your magnetic personality shines through even the cloudy days, and your belly laugh is simply contagious.

I have zero doubt that you were sent to us to bring more love, light and laughter into our lives. You've taught me to laugh off the little things, to push on for what you believe in, and how to see each day in a new light. You've also taught me immense patience and the importance of deep breaths!

You light up the room and our hearts. Shine bright, my little star.

I am one lucky Mama.

Love you beyond.

ELSA MORGAN

MAKEUP ARTIST / Mother to JASPER and JET

Sydney-based Elsa Morgan began her career as a fashion stylist, before moving to Los Angeles, where she trained as a makeup artist. She later relocated to Paris, where she worked with the likes of Balenciaga, Dior and Valentino – and met Nick, the love of her life and father of her children.

Elsa has collaborated with industry veterans including Pat McGrath, Charlotte Tilbury, the late Ashley Ward, Karim Rahman and Lucia Pieroni; worked on glossy magazines such as *Vogue*, *Harper's Bazaar*, *Elle* and *Marie Claire*; and lists such celebrities as Abby Cornish, Russell Crowe, Teresa Palmer, Wentworth Miller and Claudia Karvan as past clients. She now lives by the beach in Sydney, with her director/cinematographer husband, two energetic and adorable boys, Jet and Jasper, and Sunny the dog. "I love the daily loving that I get to be a part of," she says. "I absolutely love to play with my kids and husband, Nick, and relish all the kisses, cuddles and laughter."

222

Dear Jasper and Jet,

I was so overwhelmed with equal parts fear, joy, gratitude and panic when I discovered I was going to be a mother. I was 33 years old. You were born 18 months apart – and I hope that, because of this age gap, you will always be there for each other.

At the time, I was working as a makeup artist, living my dream of living and working in Paris. It felt important, and I was becoming the woman I was meant to be. I didn't know that meant becoming a mother! But it made sense that motherhood was always part of the journey for me. I was expressing myself as an artist and discovering new places, speaking a new language and making lifelong friends. I had never felt more free and connected with the world. Meeting your dad was the best part of this whole experience.

Working in Los Angeles and Paris, and joining teams of makeup artists who are the heroes of my industry really inspired me. They have shown me that talent has to combine with hard work, fierce determination and focus if you want to be the best.

I lived in California for six years and in Paris for four. Becoming a local is the most fun way to travel, whether you're there for a day, for a year or more. Seeing how others live and understanding another culture and language is such a challenging and exciting experience, you should embrace it whenever you can. Always make time for travel!

I was so excited to meet your dad. I thought he was French when I first met him! Then, when he switched to speaking English, I realised he was as Aussie as they come! He was so cool, relaxed and at ease with himself and the world around him. I loved that he was so carefree and fun and open. His funny, cheeky personality and love of life made him instantly – and forever – attractive to me.

With each pregnancy, I felt so protective and responsible for you both. I was so concerned for your wellbeing. When I gave birth, I missed having the control I'd felt having you tucked away safely inside my womb. But I also felt relieved that I could share the responsibility of caring for you with your dad and our family and friends.

When you were very small, everyone used to say how fast it all goes. I remember thinking, No it doesn't! This is just exhaustingly slow and hard! I was so deeply in love with you, but I was bursting to get back to 'me'. Those early days of motherhood, when I was working unpredictable hours and not earning enough to justify the help I needed, I felt frustrated. I wanted to give 100 per cent to everything in my life, but it felt impossible to be everything at once. Now that you're no longer babies, I want it all to slow down. Jasper, we've just celebrated your ninth birthday and I can't believe how quickly you've grown up.

When I became a mother, I felt like I had a different gravitational pull; my centre shifted to you both. I often felt a desperation to get to you after work. I'd race to daycare so I could be back caring for you. It was hard to balance feelings of artistic ambition with the deep instinctive need to nurture you both. I wish I'd known how much motherhood would come to redefine me. And I wish I'd known that motherhood doesn't necessarily take away from other parts of me – the parts that make me who I am. I was so scared I'd lose them.

Jet, you laugh so easily. To see you cry with laughter at the silliest things makes me melt. Jasper, you have this sly wit that comes so naturally. You're both still so happy running around the house nude. I love your cute bums flashing past me!

You're both so affectionate and I hope you always will be. Jasper, you'll reach for me and your dad when we cuddle and I see your face glow when you're in our arms. Jet, when you cuddle me at night, your body snuggles so perfectly into mine. Also, when I see you both cuddle the dog, for some reason this feels so important. This caring, unconditional love you have for Sunny and she has for you: no rules, no conversation, just warmth.

I'll continue to teach you that life is full of ups and downs. You'll learn this at school. Stay true to friends who are really there for you. Have faith that you're clever and doing your best in the moment. Be kind to yourself and allow for mistakes. I want you to be self-assured, to not take crap from people while still being a respectful person. It is a skill. It takes choosing the right words – protecting yourselves and your friends is so important.

You'll learn more about love, too. When you love someone, you'll experience feelings of joy, relief and safety. I want you to know that there's never anything lost in loving, even if it can be painful at times. How you love is who you are, no matter how the relationship goes. I believe all our loves become woven into the tapestry of our life.

Given I've spent my life working in beauty, I want to share my thoughts on beauty. The most attractive people are not the most beautiful. Remember this, always. Beauty, in an aesthetic sense, is just decorative. As with material possessions, it can be fun, but can only make you happy in a superficial way, not in the true, lasting sense.

You'll also learn about success. To me, it means a deep sense of satisfaction and achievement. This might be landing a job or something spiritual – finding peace and a sense of ease. Just work hard, play fair and never expect hand-outs. (But always take up an offer of help and show appreciation by making it mean something!) Earn and save enough and spend a little, so as not to be a burden. Enjoy and appreciate every penny you earn. Just remember, you don't have to be everything for everybody; only compare yourself to yourself.

Do I worry? All the time. I worry I might miss something or that I might try so hard I'll get in the way. I worry if I'm getting that balance right between guiding and interfering with your blossoming personalities.

I can't wait to explore the world with you, to share new cultures, food and languages with you. I'm excited to see what grabs you, what amazes you.

Always remember, there are so many more opportunities in life than at first glance. Being curious reveals more; asking boldly of yourself and the world for what you want to achieve gets you halfway there.

I'll also teach you that sometimes plans fail and you might need hindsight to understand why. Time often is the key to figuring out when something might have needed more work or a new approach, or when you might have just needed a completely new plan.

I've tried to instil in you a sense of fairness, too. We are very lucky to be Australians. I've taught you that any right you have, which you see another not enjoying, is therefore a privilege. I want you to fully enjoy this calm and free life, but without a sense of entitlement. It means we need to use our voice for those who don't have one. I hope you'll always remember me talking about gratitude. And kindness.

I've strived to be a thoughtful, respectful, empathetic, clear, light, soft, loving mother. I'm not perfect; no one is. I feel so guilty when I lose my patience; I feel embarrassed and hypocritical that I'm behaving in just the opposite way I ask of you. More than anything, I want you both to live productive, interesting, generous, creative, connected, loving, full, healthy lives. I want you to know that hard work should be embraced, not avoided. I want you to know that life can be messy, confusing and unpredictable, but the *process* of achieving your goals is part of the journey.

Be gentlemen in the truest sense. Respecting women is just another way to show you respect yourself.

My darlings, you are both what is good and true and right with the world.
Love, Mum

BOBBI BROWN

MAKEUP ARTIST, COSMETICS TYCOON and ENTREPRENEUR
Mother to DYLAN, DAKOTA and DUKE

On the day Bobbi Brown's iconic lipstick range launched at Bergdorf Goodman in 1991, she was photographed standing outside the store, proudly hugging her year-old son, Dylan.

Bobbi believes in family before anything. Throughout her career, her three sons, Dylan, Dakota and Duke (now in their 20s), have been a steady presence. She and her husband, Steven Plofker, have just celebrated 30 happy years of marriage. In 2017, she launched three new ventures – a boutique hotel in Montclair, an online editorial platform, justBOBBI.com, and a wellness line, Evolution_18. "I think my two best attributes are that I'm incredibly naive – I think it is all going to work out. I also do one thing at a time," says Bobbi. "I don't look into the future and get overwhelmed; I don't look into the past and get sad. I just try to do what is in front of me, I put one foot in front of the other and make sure I have help."

Guys,

I know you know, because I tell you all the time, how much I love you. You are my heart and soul, and I could not be prouder of the men you all are. Not that it's been easy being a working mom – especially one who gets overwhelmed by the details of life and schedules. But I am grateful that I have had the privilege of being your mom.

I also know the word 'eyeroll' is how you would sum me up. I am the mom you love to laugh at. The mom who embarrasses you by dancing on stage with Flo Rida and Salt-n-Pepa. I can't help myself, I like to have a good time. Travelling the globe and sharing these experiences with you are some of my favourite memories.

I am so glad I took you everywhere with me in my career – personal appearances, fashion shows... (even when I had 'spit up' on my back and didn't know it!).

I remember when you were growing up and had your friends over, I used to go crazy that there were 30 pairs of sneakers thrown all over the house. When you guys went to college and my house was spotless, I missed the mess. The first holiday when you were back home, the presence of 30 pairs of sneakers was so warm and comforting.

Susan Sarandon once advised me to hire a housekeeper to come on the weekends so I could take you guys to the park instead of cleaning. I regret that I didn't listen to her. I wanted the house to be perfect (it never was). I wish I'd been able to let go of the mess and embrace the chaos (I'm still working on it).

If I'd known how quickly it would go, I might have let go. But I loved all the 'chores' involved in raising you: nail cutting, baths, doctor's visits, back-to schools and travelling soccer (even though I was voted the worst soccer mom because I only brought the team orange slices and organic cookies to eat).

You know I'm over-protective and always worried about you guys from the moment you were born – the crib, the stairs, the swimming pool and crossing the street; then the cars and teenage drinking. I can't even *talk* about the Big Mountain skiing, or jumping out of planes! All I ever want is for you to be safe.

You know Dad was the big supporter of all your life experiences and, in retrospect, I'm so glad he won. You are so lucky to have him as a father; there is no bigger supporter and teacher. Your dad was always there to support us all. He even hopped on a train to Florida with four-month-old Dakota, who couldn't fly because of an ear infection, to join me and Dylan at a magazine shoot.

"*My advice to YOU ALL is... don't be afraid of failure. If you're not happy in a job, FIND A NEW one. Or better yet, be the entrepreneurs I KNOW you are.*"

As scared as I've been for your safety, I have been fearless in my work. I was raised with love and kindness, and the belief that I could do anything and be anyone. When I found makeup at university, I thought this is what I love and I want to make a career out of this. Why not? So my advice to you all is, don't think too much – just do it. Don't be afraid of failure. If you're not happy in a job, then find a new one. Or better yet, be the entrepreneurs I know you are.

Make sure that being healthy is a top priority. Feeling good and strong will allow you to be your personal best.

Lastly, what I wish for all of you is what has given me the most happiness – a happy marriage, great kids, good friends and time to enjoy them.

Love, Mom

EVA KARAYIANNIS

FOUNDER OF CARAMEL / Mother to CHLOE, KIKI and ARIS

Born in Cyprus and brought up in Athens, Eva's childhood played out by the sea with her twin brother. The family would gather on the beach and play hide-and-seek as the sun set. Trained as a lawyer, Eva started childrenswear brand Caramel 20 years ago from her kitchen table in West London, having spent two years tracking down handcrafted knitwear from Peru and clothes from individual designers in London and the Cotswolds, before opening her first shop. The label now includes womenswear and homewares.

"It seemed to me children either had to wear mass-produced clothes, or expensive glitzy items which were often impractical or anachronistic or both—none of which is what childhood is really about," explains Eva. "From the outset, I wanted to find a modern, distinctive style, which could be individual—yet at the same time luxurious and understated. That, it seems to me, is the essence of Caramel. Why shouldn't children's clothes be beautiful and tough-wearing at the same time? I like the process of creating and that's why I never stop, because it's never good enough."

Dearest Chloe, Kiki and Aris,

I have no idea if I am a good or bad mother and, to be honest, I don't even know what a good mother or a bad mother is. Chloe, when you were little, you used to say that when you grew up you would become a stay-at-home mum, one who cooked homemade meals and not just the cupcakes we occasionally baked on Saturday mornings. Which was quite amusing, because my mother never did any of the above and I still managed to find my way in life without having to see a therapist.

Recently, you, Chloe (at age 23) congratulated me on being *me*. So perhaps the lesson is that we shouldn't hold up a stereotype of what a mother is, because it makes life stressful and confusing. Every mother can be different and choose a way that works for her to bring up her children.

What else will help you navigate your life better? First and foremost, discover your sense of self. The sooner you decide what you wish to do with your life and what makes you tick, the better. That way, you can work out your own rules in all aspects of life: how to be a partner, husband/wife/mother/father, career person. Granted, this is not something that you will necessarily understand until much later.

It's also important to choose your partner wisely. Strive for an equal relationship (in all areas) and try to allow people to be themselves. Remember, it's partnership rather than ownership and you're in marriage for the long game. Bringing up a family is a collaboration; it wasn't me doing everything at home. You need to do things as a family, a team. When your father was working in a more demanding job, I had to do school pick-ups and be around more. Then the roles reversed, which, for our generation, was a very modern approach.

Growing up, I was fortunate enough never to have felt that I had to go and get a specific job. Even when I trained as a lawyer and then went on to become a childrenswear designer, my parents didn't judge. So make life choices that allow you to have a profession you enjoy in the long term. My achievement is that I have a life in place which allows me to have continuous pleasure. Remember, too, to enjoy the process. This is very important.

It has been a conscious decision not to have investors in Caramel and consequently have to report to them, which means I have 12 stores worldwide and not 140. In business, I've learnt it's better to be gentle (although this is different from being a doormat), because when you are kind, you get the most out of your team. I have a good work ethic and I like to think I have led by example.

I think it's important to understand that things around you (hopefully) come from a place of integrity. Learn to appreciate quality and care about what you consume, because when you understand and appreciate what you have, then you will become happy, fulfilled, stronger and grounded.

What has motherhood taught me? That you experience life in a far richer way, even if it actually makes you poorer! You also get quicker at everything.

Don't wrap up your own children in cotton wool, they will never learn to deal with the hurley-burley that comes their way if you have spoonfed them everything. They need to build up resilience and learn to go with the flow.

Also, don't get too caught up with what a 'successful' childhood looks like and focus instead on raising someone who is compassionate and kind. Mothers put so much pressure on themselves and, in the end, the academia, the schooling, which friendships to have... Well, they don't really matter. Motherhood is also about priorities: what do you prioritise in life and what do you let slide?

It's a cliché, but don't sweat the small stuff. Because the superwoman myth is exactly that. A myth.

Love from Mummy

> *"Discover your SENSE of SELF. The sooner you decide what YOU WISH to do with your LIFE and what makes you tick, the better."*

FIONA MYER

FASHION DESIGNER / Mother to ED, WILL and JESS

Fiona Myer, entrepreneur amd art patron, modelled in Paris before working as a fashion forecaster. After her three children were born, the family moved to Malaysia for nearly five years. There, she worked with artisans around the region, designing products such as linen from Vietnam and wicker furniture from Myanmar.

Returning to Australia, Fiona went on to co-launch the fashion label White Story in 2015. The initial range was founded on the principles of simplicity and purity – a desire to move back to basics. Inspired by her passion for ceramics, architecture, fashion, contemporary art and all things white, Fiona's brand is defined by its attention to detail and emphasis on tailoring.

And, while her three children have all left home now, they reunite often at their family farm – a spectacular 16-hectare retreat 45 kilometres outside Melbourne.

Darling Will, Ed and Jess,

I am writing to you from the pool house at the farm – the place you know I love. For once, the music is turned down to a whisper, as I sit and contemplate my life and my advice as a mother to the three of you.

Before I start my journey on paper, I want you to know that, individually and collectively, you make my life worth living. I feel blessed to have brought you into this world, into my life, and I can't imagine a life without you.

If I have forgotten to tell you, you are my best friends, the ones I can trust and rely on, and, most of all, have fun with. No amount of distance will ever pull us apart.

As you know, I have always said life is a journey, not a destination. Don't wait for the right time to say something or the right time to change direction in your life. You are your own destiny.

Life is hard to explain and even harder to analyse – to know what's right and what's wrong. I have spent my life trusting my gut instinct. It's not always been right, but in the main, it has stood me in good stead.

You have all, in your own ways, taught me more about myself and I thank you for this. My hope is that, as your loving mother, I can leave you with some advice along the way that won't change your life but might colour your views. It's the stuff we can't see in life. It's the energy between two people that matters. As they say, the context of a good speech may be forgotten, but what will be remembered is the way you made people feel.

To be honest, frank and transparent are values I hold dear to myself. I am, however, still learning the art of not being too blunt!

Ever since I was a little girl, I wanted to be included. These days, it's called FOMO. My advice here is that you can't be everybody's best friend. Spend time being a good listener to those who matter and don't be afraid to give advice. As they say, advice is free, whether worthless or priceless!

I have learnt that you can't really do more than one job at a time and give it your best. I have found over my life, there have been so many things I've wanted to achieve that, at times, I became scattered.

White Story has taught me to stay focused. It is my hope that you three can see that, while it is challenging, it is possible to start an embryonic business at any age. It feeds my soul and makes me feel worthwhile. It's what gets me out of bed in the morning, while you are all away on your journeys.

However, one thing that remains constant – family comes first. Dad and the three of you have my unconditional love and attention. I want you to know I will drop anything to come to your rescue. A phone call away for advice; a big hug and a full-bodied red if we are together!

In life, everything can be resolved. It usually starts with a conversation. Don't hold things in. Talk about them, uneasy as you may be. Break up the word 'disease' and you get 'dis-ease'. This is what happens when the mind and the body are not at ease with one another.

Be trusting – most people have good intentions. We can all go through life being wary and trusting no one. This is disheartening and leaves you feeling alone and even in despair.

My life has been colourful and I feel I have achieved a lot. I am forever grateful for that. They say I'm lucky, but I say you make your own luck. I found what I was passionate about after I left school. Not being good at everything makes the process of elimination a lot easier!

The choices you all have today are endless. Be true to yourself and make sure that whatever you decide to do with your career you are at least 85 per cent happy. If not, change direction. This is not a dress rehearsal and as surely as one door closes, another one opens.

This goes for relationships, too. If you are not more than 85 per cent happy, then have a good look at yourself. Don't rely on your partner to provide your happiness. Happiness needs to come from within. Your friend, lover, wife or husband should be your best friend. That's the cream.

As you know, Dad and I celebrated 33 years of marriage last month. I say that knowing we had a little three-month blip… No one's life is perfect, but life is what we make of it.

A favourite mantra of mine is 'You are the company you keep'. So if you're not sure about someone in your business life or personal life, then steer clear of them. Surround yourself with like-minded people who are uplifting and make you smile.

Mistakes? I've made a few. Our nearly five years in Malaysia was a gutsy thing to do and left us with wonderful memories of our lives overseas. But if I had my time again I would have resisted the temptation of having *amahs* [nursemaids]. I am hugely regretful that, despite our best intentions, the amahs snatched our most precious years together. When we came back to Australia, the amahs followed us. Although we spent *almost* all the time together, it wasn't *all* the time together.

Once a mother, always a mother. Slipping into the expat life meant that you, Ed, started school aged two. Although it felt strange, it was the way of life. Not to have you by my side and in my arms at such a young age was a huge regret for me. The upside now is your ability to socialise and build relationships, and get on with people.

Ed, you will stay in my mind forever when you stopped in the street. You were in year nine and asked me, "What do I have to do to live the life that you and Dad live?" Startled and surprised, I said, "Stay hungry."

I feel incredibly proud to say that all three of you are truly hungry. You have completely blown Dad and me away with what you've all achieved.

Ed, darling, you were always the funny one, the one we could rely on to keep us smiling. Don't forget that. If you are not smiling and joking each day, ask yourself why.

Jess, darling, girls and mothers share a bond that can't really be explained. There really is nothing on earth we don't talk about, is there. Granny would be forever proud to see our beautiful relationship. You are wise beyond your years. You are my go-to person during tricky times, and I know I can confide in you to offer me an honest yet compassionate opinion. Darling, did I ever tell you that you are one of the funniest people I have ever met? Our trip to Japan will last a lifetime of funny memories.

Will, darling, you are my eldest child, with a steady hand. You are wise counsel and I know I can always trust and rely on you, even if you are slow to get back on WhatsApp! When I think of you, I think of the book *Leaders Eat Last*. You are resilient and patient. You have found yourself in some rare situations, but kept a cool head and I know this will see you through your life. If I had a dollar for everyone who says they love Will, I might retire early!

To 'have someone's back' is the greatest compliment. To know you all have each other's back, as well as Dad's and mine, is hugely comforting.

Finally, I know I'm a nag, but Christmas is Christmas! You know my line 'Those that play together, stay together'. Please guys, I know it's a huge journey for you all, but if we can't all be in the same place for birthdays, then Christmas is non-negotiable. Please can we all be together. So, WhatsApp me on our Family Banter with a yes. *Please.*

All my love always, Mum

RACHELLE HRUSKA MACPHERSON

FOUNDER of LINGUA FRANCA and GUEST OF A GUEST
Mother to MAXWELL and DASHIELL

What do you get when you mix hip-hop lyrics with ethical cashmere sweaters? Rachelle Hruska MacPherson's clever and stylish take on the current political climate, mixing symbolic messages of hope and humour with a touch of activism. Lingua Franca knitwear's point of difference is all in the hand-embroidered slogans created by Rachelle to start essential conversations in scary political times. Rachelle is also the brains behind social website Guest of a Guest, a digital media database of global cultural events.

If you're getting the vibe that Rachelle is a consummate multitasker, you're not wrong. With the help of her husband, Sean, and the unparalleled love that comes with being a mother to two sons, Maxwell and Dashiell, she has not only achieved commercial success but also overcome often debilitating anxiety and panic attacks. The story of how Lingua Franca helped her through dark times is fascinating and inspirational.

Boys,

Your favourite song to have me sing you before bedtime is Leonard Cohen's *Hallelujah*, and it delights me every time. I'm moved that such a heavy ballad, packed with nuanced expressions of what it means to be alive and in love, speaks to you. Things in life aren't black and white; they're complicated and heartbreaking. But they are also beautiful.

It's hard for me to get into the *big* questions with you both right now – where we came from and what happens to us when we die – partly because you're too young to grasp these concepts fully, but also because I'm still working through them myself. Hopefully, you will study philosophical and theological theories in depth to seek a faith that speaks to you. But for now, Leonard Cohen seems to sum it up best for us.

Which is where I come to my first piece of advice: take inspiration from anywhere and everywhere. You can find poetry in Hallmark cards and lullabies in pop culture songs.

My next piece of friendly advice is: be you. One of the hardest things I've done in my life was to truly learn how to listen to myself. It sounds silly – shouldn't we know who we are just by being in our own bodies? For whatever reason, it will seem much easier to listen to others than it will be to stop and listen to your own heart. You must, and I mean *must*, learn to love yourself and listen to your inner voice. It is hard. It takes practice. It takes a real desire from within. It will be scary and painful at times, and it won't always steer you in the right direction. But if you listen to other people's ideas of how you should live or who you ought to become, you will miss out on one of the greatest joys in life: being you.

Don't be afraid of pain. Experiencing true heartache is one of those things that will make you feel truly alive. There's a line I read I always return to: 'The gift is in the wound.' Gorgeous, right? Or, take it from Leonard Cohen: 'There is a crack, a crack in everything, that's how the light gets in.' In short, embrace the pain. You will love and you will lose. But never stay in a place that isn't right for you just because you are afraid of the unknown.

Take who you are and what you do in life seriously. You're fortunate to have your basic needs met. This means you owe it to the universe to try to use your talents for good while staying true to your inner joys. Find out what you love to do and make it your number-one goal to make it your life's work. The world will be a better place if you succeed.

On the other hand, *don't* take who you are or what you do too seriously. When things get nutty, I like to remember that we're all going to die someday and in 100 years' time, there'll be all new people roaming the streets. I'm proud of my companies and am deeply invested in my work, but at the end of my life, I'll be thinking of the victories of my heart. You and your father are my life's best work. You're my greatest joys and my truest loves. At my end, I'll be holding onto the small moments I had with you. The memories we write down together in our personal history books make up the most important parts of me.

Find the humour in anything and everything. Appreciate the absurdity. A trick I've learnt on days I'm feeling blue is to remind myself that scientific studies have confirmed there are more good people than bad on our planet. More random acts of kindness happen each day than acts of destruction. They just don't make the news.

Be quirky and be kind. I adore characters who are considerate. Who doesn't? Remember the words of Aretha Franklin: Respect. Respect your body, respect yourself, respect others, respect the planet. Respect: keep asking for it and keep giving it. Always, generously.

Finally, remember this, no one knows what they're doing. For real! Isn't that liberating?! We're all just out here trying our best. Remind yourself of this when you come across adversaries. Even bullies need love. Especially bullies.

Boys, I loved you even before I met you. I shouted Hallelujah! the day you were born. I will always love you unconditionally. Know this as you make your way in the world and keep it as a magic tool to use. You're lucky to have each other, so have each other's backs, always. Be true to yourself and friendly to others. As long as I'm alive, I'll be forever yours.

I did my best, it wasn't much
I couldn't feel, so I tried to touch
I've told the truth, I didn't come to fool you
And even though it all went wrong
I'll stand before the lord of song
With nothing on my tongue but Hallelujah
Hallelujah, Hallelujah, Hallelujah, Hallelujah
Mama xo

CLEMMIE HOOPER

MIDWIFE and AUTHOR
Mother to ANYA, MARNIE, OTTILIE and DELILAH

Clemmie Hooper will make you smile. That's a given. A mother to four girls (check out her Instagram account @mother_of_daughters), she knows a thing or two about giving birth and shares her knowledge with warmth and authenticity. "Apparently, I was always interested in babies, even as a little girl, and as soon as I understood what a midwife was, I decided I wanted to be one!" she says.

Clemmie lives by the sea in Kent in England, with her four girls and husband Simon, who is possibly one of the funniest men on Instagram (have a look, too, at his feed @father_of_daughters). On being a mother of four (including twins), she says, "Just watching the four of them together, despite the age gaps, they all really love each other. Now the twins are much more fun and playful, the older girls love taking on that big-sister role. Our house is very noisy and crazy, but I wouldn't have it any other way."

A letter to my daughters, Anya, Marnie, Ottilie and Delilah

To my wonderful, beautiful, fiery girls, I've penned you this letter to give you the tools you need to embark on becoming women. Although that feels like a long way away, I want you to have some words of wisdom from me, your Mama, that I think might help you along the way. Some advice may seem completely irrelevant and trivial to you now, but I promise you will thank me in your own ways.

Being a woman is an amazing thing. It can feel complicated, frustrating and at times unfair (for instance, why don't men have to deal with periods?), but you have such an exciting life ahead of you. I'm excited for you!

• Getting up and going to school every day may seem like a chore, but the stuff you're going to learn, the friendships you'll form and the experiences you'll gain are invaluable for the 'real world'. You will also look back and be grateful for having a school uniform. Having to decide what to wear to work each day is stressful and requires some night-before, anxiety-induced planning.

• There'll be some things you have to learn in maths and science for your GCSEs that you will never have to use in your adult life. But just learn them, write them down a thousand times on Post-it notes, then, once your exams are over, you'll never again have to think about the geometric progression of a number sequence.

• And while on the subject of education, all I ask is that you try not to worry too much about what you want to be when you're grown up. Not many people know, and you don't even have to go to university if it's not the right thing for you. I will support you, whatever you choose to do. My only tip is to make sure you have the passion and fire in your belly for whatever job you end up doing. It helps when your alarm goes off at 6am every day to know you're going to do a job you love.

• Female friendships are wonderful and complicated, but essential for getting through life. You'll have big fall-outs over matters that feel really important, but often, once the dust has settled and the tears have dried, it's time to make up. Hug, learn to apologise and never lose a friend over a boy.

• Which brings me to love. Falling in love is the most amazing feeling, and everyone should be lucky enough to experience those 'butterflies in the stomach'. You may fall in love many times; it may only happen once. But when your heart is broken, it hurts more than any other pain. And you'll cry, sob, weep, punch your pillow and scream with rage because it's so unfair. I've experienced this once. You never forget how it feels. Your heart is a precious thing, so look after it and never accept being second best.

• Always invest in a decent bra fitted by a professional. If you're lucky (unlucky?) enough to have my big boobs, you'll soon realise that cheap bras do not cut the mustard. You'll end up chucking them out. Buy cheap, buy twice.

• Your body is the most beautiful body in the world. You have arms and legs that work and allow you to do incredible things. But we are living in a society that expects women to look a certain way. Many of those images you'll see in the media are unrealistic; they've been edited to make you believe that's how you should look. Love your body, thank it every day for what it allows you to do and remember that diets never work long-term. Starving yourself because of an image you've seen has huge consequences for your self-worth.

• You have all been blessed with wonderful thick eyebrows. Don't over-pluck them, because they will never grow back the way you want them to.

• No matter what time you go to sleep, always take off your makeup. You'll be thankful in the morning.

• And make your bed every day: getting into a made bed in the evening is really good for the mind.

• Learn to make three basic meals – spaghetti with homemade tomato sauce, an omelette, and baked beans on toast with grated cheese.

• Fill your home with flowers and music. We always play great tunes for our regular kitchen discos and have fresh flowers on the table. Both will make you feel bloody happy.

• You are all so lucky to each have three sisters – they will be your best friends and know you better than anyone else. Call them!

• You will experience rejection and disappointment; it's part of life. It doesn't feel great, but it's good for you to remember that sometimes things aren't right for you, right now. Learn from it, get feedback and move on.

• Manners and kindness cost nothing. I know you all roll your eyes when I tell you to sit properly at the table or remind you to say thank you, but it is important. Try and do one kind act a day: it can be as small as holding the door open for someone behind you. You never know how your actions might make someone's day.

• Sometimes, asking yourself what's the worst that can happen can help you make some pretty big decisions. Not that many things are permanent; even tattoos can be removed (although I hear it's really painful and expensive). So don't get a crap tattoo at 18 when you go travelling.

• I am a firm believer in 'if it's meant to be...' Sometimes trusting the universe is enough. You are enough.

• You are all as wonderfully different from each other as sisters can be. Being your mother has filled me with a new level of understanding of how complex, yet remarkable, girls are. And one day, if you are all lucky enough to become mothers, I hope you get more sleep than I did and understand why I'd sometimes hide in the bathroom eating chocolate and scrolling through Instagram, just to have five minutes' peace.

With all my love, Mama

LARA EINZIG

FOUNDER of AQUADORIUM / Mother to RAPHAEL, LOUIS and FLYNN

Meet Lara Einzig, an Aussie-raised, LA-based mother of three with an impressive fashion industry background at Topshop and Goop, where she was fashion director. Her business, Aquadorium, celebrates the sun-kissed beach lifestyle through personal styling, creative direction, content curation and brand collaborations. Lara grew up "free range" near the beach in Queensland and, after spending years in Sydney and London, she is now living the beachside dream in LA with her husband, Dan, and their sons.

Lara is disarmingly self-effacing and honest: "Gwyneth [Paltrow] interviewed me at her home in London six weeks after the twins arrived," she recalls. "I used so many breast pads that day, terrified that I'd start leaking during the interview!"

Lara is the kind of spirit mama you want in your corner. Whether it's her advice on looking your best or just being honest about the reality of motherhood, she's a total inspiration. "It's not about being mother of the year – sometimes that feeling of just trying to survive is ok, and it's 100 per cent ok to talk about that."

Dear Raphael, Louis and Flynn,

What a truly beautiful and unexpected journey we've been on together over the past few years. Raphael, you're now eight years old, and Louis and Flynn, both five. It feels like the perfect time to take a moment and deeply reflect on these wonderful years. I absolutely cherish being your mummy.

But to my surprise and utter devastation, motherhood did not come easily for me. Failing month after month, year after year at something I was born to do, my whole purpose in life. It was truly one of the most difficult traumas I've ever experienced. The pure elation and gratitude I felt when I found out I was pregnant (for both pregnancies) was just euphoric. I was about to have what I'd wanted most in the world and I went on to really enjoy beautiful pregnancies with you all.

I absolutely loved when you were all babies. The marvel of newborns was just so divine and unexpected. Of course, the early weeks turned our lives upside down, but if I had the chance to do it all again, I would in a heartbeat.

Ralphy, when you were born, I just remember feeling pure obsession towards you. I couldn't get enough of you. When you were sleeping, I would pore over pictures of you and when you were awake, I would stare at your face for hours, just overwhelmingly grateful, with a raw and deeply beautiful understanding of eternal love.

Flynn and Louis, when you arrived, I honestly don't remember much! Life more than turned upside-down; it exploded! But I loved it and, just when I thought I couldn't love anything more, you both instantly expanded my heart. I do remember waking in the mornings to find our bedroom in an absolute state of chaos – bottles everywhere, nappies and dirty muslins strewn, breast pumps, toys, dirty pyjamas, gripe water, dummies, wet wipes – almost every surface littered with baby paraphernalia. In those early days, every morning was like surfacing from a baby bomb site – shock, surveying the devastation, exhaustion, happy to be alive! Luckily, Grandma Juju was always there to help pick up the pieces.

After you all arrived, we slowed everything down. We lived in central London and I was always rushing around. When I gave birth to you, Ralphy, I was terrified of dropping you or falling down the stairs with you. The fear and anxiety were overcoming me. Then, one day, your grandfather said rather profoundly, "Just don't be in a rush and you won't have an accident." I still need to remind myself to slow down and I think I'm occasionally sent little signs and reminders to ease up.

Time has flown at lightning speed and even faster now you're all at school. Each new phase is so fascinating; I'm always looking forward to what's next. Those big transitions to preschool and then school leave me nostalgic, with an overwhelming feeling of sadness that my little ones are quickly growing up. I have recently discovered that, in the context of our lives, you are in our hands and our homes for such a short time before you leave the nest. To me, this is devastating and I wish time would slow down just a little.

Louis and Flynn, I love that you're so protective of each other and truly the best of friends. Your elder brother, Ralphy, is your hero and I love how well you play together and how much you genuinely love each other.

Ralphy, you are so deliciously innocent and honest. You're such a happy boy and it's so easy for you to make new friends wherever you go – I love that confidence. Please don't stop writing me love letters – you must have got this from your daddy. It makes me so happy.

Flynn, you're a born entertainer and light up every room – don't worry, my love, we'll find a way for you to sing on stage! And I love that you always comment on my "beautiful" dresses.

Louis the love-bug, you're a builder and monster-truck lover and happily share your passion with others, but you're equally content playing all day by yourself. I love how strong and competitive you are – your refusal to lose – but also how you sweetly mirror Flynn's feelings. If Flynn is sick, you are, too!

I'm striving to simply be the best mother I can be. I'm not following any books or guidelines; I'm making this up as I go by constantly being close to you, observing, being intuitive and fuelling your bodies and minds. Of course, I want to give you everything you need and desire, but I also want to continue to teach you to fend for yourselves and find your own way.

Flynn and Louis, we moved to LA when you were 18 months old; Ralphy, you were four. It was a difficult time. We didn't know anyone, we had no support and your dad was building a business from the ground up and regularly flying back to London. Meanwhile, I was struggling with the grief of losing my beloved little sister, your Auntie Julia, back in Australia. It was a huge low point in my motherhood journey, because I truly believed I was a terrible mother, and in the stress of it all, I got quite ill.

On reflection, everything I was doing was for you boys. I was trying to make a lovely new home for you. I realised later that I wasn't a terrible mother; I was doing my best and you were happy! I just wasn't able to feel happy because of the grief I was experiencing.

Taking time for myself away from the family – surrounding myself with nature, keeping fit and healthy – gave me strength. I found surfing an incredible emotional outlet for me – it's meditative and physically challenging, my happy place. I'm hoping that one day it will be yours, too.

Ralphy, when you were 11 months old, I happily went back to work and you happily took it in your stride. Again, managing work stress was difficult, but the change in my efficiency was so interesting – something just kicked in and took over. Your focus is suddenly pin-sharp because, suddenly, your one priority is getting the job done and getting home as quickly as possible.

Louis and Flynn, when you were four months old, after much soul-searching, I took on a new role that ultimately wasn't for me, prompting me to take a step back from my career. You all needed me more than I needed to feel like a career woman. There was plenty of time for that. My belief is that our family is not going to work if both parents have demanding careers and are never around, which is why I'm building my own business on my terms. Ultimately, I'm doing this for us.

Daddy and I want you to grow up in a world fuelled by love and democracy, tolerance and patience in an environment that is being protected and restored. By being educated, worldly, compassionate, curious and observant, you will have the tools you need to stand up for what's important. Boys, we have a big job ahead of us. We need to engage and activate to truly make a difference. I know we can do it!

Our beautiful boys, Ralphy, Flynn and Louis, since coming into our lives you have, quite simply, made everything better, more exciting, more meaningful, more joyful. You've made us feel love in a more profound way than we could have ever felt on our own. You've challenged us and our lives in more ways than we could have imagined, but this has been the driving force in making our lives together so exciting. You've taught us so much about ourselves – our strengths, values, failures. You've given us a phenomenal insight into the world when we look at it through your eyes. We want you to live a life that is balanced, healthy, rewarding, adventurous, passionate, informed, dynamic, and full of love and laughter; to have the natural ability to offset highs and lows. But ultimately, we have learnt this pure truth – happiness and love are all that matters.

Auntie Kaz sent me this beautiful poem before I first became a mother and I want to share it with you boys, because I feel every word in my heart about each of you. I don't know who wrote it, but it always makes me cry and it will continue to stay with me forever.

Before you were conceived I wanted you. Before you were born I loved you. Before you were an hour old, I would die for you. This is the miracle of life.

Love, Mum

EMMA LANE

CO-OWNER of THE FARM at BYRON BAY
Mother to CHARLIE, GEORGE, MATILDA and LULU

The inspired sustainable produce and restaurant concept, The Farm in Byron Bay, was co-created by Emma Lane with husband Tom, heir to the Oroton fashion empire. The motto 'Grow. Feed. Educate. Give Back' could be translated to all aspects of the idyllic family life they've created in the Byron Bay hinterland. This 80-acre working farm is a legacy project with community at its heart, educating people about sustainability and delivering real, delicious food following the 'paddock to plate' philosophy. Whatever produce isn't cultivated on the farm is sourced locally.

Driven by the desire to teach their children about real food and a love of the land, Emma and Tom gave up other work commitments – Emma from the world of advertising and Tom from his family business – which prompted their 'tree change' move from Sydney. However, the dream life that Emma has created for her family has meant plenty of introspection, changes of course and sheer hard work. Whether it's about fertility or holistic health, she has inspiring tales to share about creating and sustaining a healthy, harmonious family life.

Emma knows only too well that life isn't always shiny and bright. "You may look at my four healthy children, all close in age, and deduce the journey of pregnancy has been easy for us. It took 11 pregnancies to have four children," she says.

Dear beautiful offspring, Charlie, George, Matilda and Lulu,

I sit here while I pen this letter, looking out across the rolling hills of Byron Bay with a full heart, reflecting on motherhood and life. I acknowledge the part you play in this ancestry adventure. I thank you for trusting me to steer you across the temperamental waters of growing up and for your part in crafting the mother in me. From you, I have learnt so much about so many things. You've taught me patience and kindness, about uncertainty and, of course, about the power of unconditional love. Among these words, I offer you some thoughts and insights on what I've learnt so far, in life and as a mother. I hope you choose what you need to take with you through your life.

My maternal instinct didn't kick in early and I often wonder if that was due to losing my own mother at the age of nine (your age now, my dear Matilda). She was only 32 when a boating accident took away her last breath on a return trip from France. Your grandfather lived to tell the tale, but sadly, I had far too many questions left for her that have remained unanswered.

I often wonder what kind of mother she would have been, what insights I would have gained from her nurturing and what I inherited naturally from her. Was I like her? What would she have done in my maternal shoes? Questions popped up regularly in the early mothering years, until one day I tapped into my intuition – the universal mothering instinct. In this space, I discovered that I already had the answers within me; I just needed to trust myself.

With that, I give you the first lesson: Trust your instincts and believe that the answers you seek in life are already there deep in your heart.

Not having my natural mother around, I often wonder if I missed valuable lessons about motherhood that I might have absorbed from simply watching her. Just being in her company, I might have gained motherly insights as second nature. Instead, I started with a completely clean slate, navigating parenting in uncharted waters. At times, there's no denying it was a passage of whitewater rapids, but among the rough waters, there was also plenty of calm, when the sparkling sunlight shone beautifully on the water's crystal surface. We've experienced many little rays of joy shining bright in our life. We are all riding the waves, each of us taking our turn at the helm, because we are all in this together, learning valuable lessons from each other.

I continue to learn as much from you as I hope you do from me. I have sometimes relied on others for support, when four little people running around became overwhelming, and that's ok. There are many people in life from whom we can learn. You don't have to learn all the lessons yourselves.

So, lesson two: Be open to asking for help. We are all here to carry the load together. As you've heard me and others say before, it takes a village to raise a child. We are not in this alone.

Motherhood is a delicate balance of trial and error, and it was during pregnancy that I would learn the next two lessons I would like to share with you. They are simple, but hold abiding value. On the back of a fast-paced career in advertising, I had forgotten how to slow down and this kept me in a hectic state of 'flight or fight'. After several miscarriages, I knew I had to change the pace, if not for me, then for you. I needed to create a soft and nurturing environment for my little people to grow. So, I learnt to slow down and to breathe again; to trust in myself and to be soft. The reward was you.

So, lesson three: Do not exist in a state of stress. If life is not going your way, don't tighten the grip, loosen it. Slow down and reconnect body, mind and spirit. Observe the ways that calm your system and ground you, whether it's walking in nature, meditation or talking it out with friends. Follow your instincts – you will be shown the way.

Along with calm breath, your other most valuable life-force currency is real food. In the quest to create the best life for you, I turned to food to nourish our family. From what we learnt, we created The Farm at Byron Bay. Born from our own experience of growing real food, our purpose became a mission to educate others about wellness from the ground up. The Farm is now a place for people to wander, to learn about where food comes from, and to encourage community.

Lesson four: Eat food as close to nature as possible. We are what we eat. Enjoy food as close to its natural state as possible and you will be on the right track to nourish your body to be the best version of yourself.

Lesson five: Have a purpose and set goals you want to achieve for yourself and for the world which might benefit others. It's good to have something bigger than you – it's a way to give back and show gratitude for the fortunate lives we lead. Your father and I believe that working on projects with a social conscience is our way to give back. In your career, try not to just focus on monetary return.

Our hope for the future is that we can leave the planet a bit better than when we arrived, and if we can attempt to give back in some way, we will feel more fulfilled with our existence.

There have been times in my life when I lost my way a little. It helps to figure out early how to walk to the beat of your own drum. Live your life how you want to live it, not how you feel others expect you to. Even in motherhood, others will try to tell you the way it should be done.

To know yourself and what you want from life will help you to make the right decisions in all areas. You may meet people along the way who try to lead you off track, particularly when you are shining bright. Not everyone wants to see you shine and not everyone will see the true beauty in you. You need to learn when to walk away from those who are not serving you well.

Lesson six: Take time to know yourself and stay strong and true to this. You are perfect, my loves, just as you are.

Lesson seven: Navigate with kindness. The old saying about treating others how you would be treated yourself will serve you well. Sometimes, you will be challenged by difficult people and experience mean and unkind behaviour. Understand that everyone has a story and a reason for why they behave as they do. If you come from a position of empathy, and don't take their behaviour personally, you can navigate without the heaviness of guilt. With that grace we can travel further, higher and with a fuller heart.

My little loves, this life is here to enjoy. So, seize it with both hands and your whole being. It's with lightness we want to travel on this life journey, locking away any unecessary emotional baggage in the smallest suitcase. Somehow, if we can stay connected to our inner child, we can remain playful and live abundantly, open to enjoying all the beautiful qualities of happiness. Laugh, be silly, jump, skip, be creative and the inevitable burdens of life will not keep you down for long.

You continue to show me the joy of this innocent playfulness. Looking through yours, I see again with beginner's eyes. I thank you for all this, and for the tears of both frustration and joy in motherhood. Most of all, I thank you for helping me stay connected to the child in me, because that little person in all of us is born happy and to be loved. It really is very simple.

With motherhood, everything has changed and I am more me than I have ever been. I thank you all for those blessings, my little loves.

Forever your mother, I love you. x

PIPPA SMALL

JEWELLERY DESIGNER and ACTIVIST / Mother to MAC and MADELEINE

The more you learn about Pippa Small, the more impressive her list of achievements. She was awarded an MBE for ethical jewellery production and her charity work, teamed up with Tom Ford for Gucci, and became an ambassador for Survival International (a cause that fights for land rights for indigenous peoples). She is also a single mother to twins Mac and Madeleine.

"I had the twins at 43, after trying for many years to have a baby," says Pippa.
"I had faced the possibility of not having children and that made me very sad. So, ever since the twins arrived healthy and perfect, I have been in a place of gratitude.
The sleeplessness of the early days felt like a small challenge."
Pippa grew up in Northern Quebec in Canada, in a large family she describes as being both "a joy" and, at times, "overwhelming". As a child, she loved to read and found solace in stones, imbuing them with memories and emotions. Her life since has been a rich tapestry of adventure, activism and anthropology, as she travels the world helping to drive positive change wherever she can.

Dear ones,

I'm writing this letter in a room in the hills of Corsica, the doors open to the small balcony overooking the green hills and out to sea. You two are playing in the other room, chatting in your made-up languages, collecting fruit and flowers from the garden and placing them in patterns on the floor.

I've never known such peace and deep sense of wellbeing as in these past six years since you were born. I've been so joy-filled and full of gratitude.

We all make choices in life, sometimes subconsciously, often nudged by fear to be safe or by convention; or, at times, driven by challenges, by curiosity. My choices were likely reflections of my childhood, a tree with so many branches of people and places that have inspired and nudged me on my journey. Now I look for clues as to what you might do with your lives.

I grew up in an unconventional family: four marriages produced eight children spanning two generations. My father was old enough to be my great-grandfather, and people often thought my mother was my grandmother. We are a tangle of generations, of aunts younger than their nieces, a family scattered across continents.

Being the youngest, I was quiet, watchful and shy, finding it safer to be invisible among the noise and tumble of a big family. I lived in a world inside my head, seeking the company of animals and the outdoors. I read voraciously and grew to understand the world through the animals I spent time with, the books I read, and complex family dynamics. But my strength came from nature, sitting in trees observing the natural world. There, I found peace and sense.

My father passed away when I was eight and my life stood still for a long time. Though he'd been distant, I was his favourite and the loss left me more shut off. I carried my grief in bracelets I made from his buttons and cufflinks. More loss was to follow – moves away from those I loved and felt safe with, moves of country. The stones I collected from beaches and riverbeds brought comfort and stability. I'd carry around pocketfuls of rocks, smooth pebbles and odd beads and gems from family members. I started turning them into jewellery, just to be able to carry them close and not lose them. The bracelets that adorned my wrists like a Masai's were a tactile diary of my existence.

After my father died, my mother decided at last she could do the things she wanted. Travel was one of her dreams. With her three younger children, she took us to desert festivals in North Africa, palaces in India and ancient ruins in Turkey. A favourite memory is of her dancing with an old shepherd in the firelight, arms in the air and whirling to an accordion at a wedding in Anatolia.

We went to Tanzania, where the Masai fascinated me. I wanted to know how they lived, how they saw the world, what they believed in, how they lived off that beautiful land. In Morocco, I wanted to join a family of Berber farmers as they rode off on their donkeys after the weekly market, back to their hilltop villages in the Atlas Mountains.

This fascination for peoples who lived in faraway places – their way of life dictated by the landscape and their interdependence with the natural world – started to shape my life. I wanted to understand their traditions, the rules that dictated their lives, the gods they worshipped and the poetry they spoke.

At university, I found I loved learning. I studied anthropology and it entranced me, but I still carried a sense of what it is to be invisible, to be unheard, to have no voice. I gravitated towards human rights, in particular the rights of indigenous peoples – tribal communities silenced by nation states, their languages and the knowledge contained within banned – who were losing their land. I went to work in northern Borneo and felt at last a sense of purpose, an excitement at being alive.

From that time in my early 20s, as I started to travel the world on my own, living and working with remote communities in the rainforest in the highlands of the Philippines and Thailand, I knew I wanted to share these remarkable experiences with my children. I wanted them to celebrate the diversity of this beautiful world. To sit at the feet of wise elders and learn how to find balance, to live harmoniously in the world; to find a mentor as I did with Lui the Naga, a

human rights activist and great humanitarian I worked with. I wanted them to understand the deeper meanings of our world, the ancientness, the beauty, the continuity, the respect for nature I felt in these traditional communities.

As working with NGOs turned to a more researched-based role, I could see a void in working with communities to generate income. I began working with the San bushmen in the Kalahari in Botswana, creating traditional craft but designed with a contemporary feel and style. I went on to work in many beautiful places and with inspiring people in Rwanda, Kenya, Panama, Chile, Bolivia, South Africa, Afghanistan and India.

In every place, I was so filled with excitement and awe at the places and people and life stories I was gathering. But my longing for a child grew. I wanted to feel a part of this greater humanity by sharing that journey of motherhood. My relationships, while wonderful and enriching, never seemed to be with someone who shared this desire. As the years passed, I tried hard to meditate and accept that I might never have a child.

But I couldn't let go of this dream. I made up my mind at 38 that, while falling in love could happen with the right man at any age, a child was not something I could leave to fate. So I started the long, difficult journey of IVF as a single mother. I went to clinics, doctors, hospitals; endured endless needles, drugs, tests, hopes, fears. Five miscarriages, eight rounds of IVF and finally a successful pregnancy. When they told me I was carrying twins, I was overjoyed, and the fact that you were a girl and a boy could not have been more perfect.

Although my pregnancy was mostly angst-filled, I loved carrying you, loved growing larger and having you there with me at every moment. It felt like a miracle after so many years of longing, of consulting every witch and holy shrine and altar, of gathering every fertility amulet and praying every day.

During this time, a friend came to my rescue and became more. He came to doctors' appointments, he helped me put on my shoes when I could no longer reach my feet, he stayed to be there at your birth and grew to love you, too. Suddenly, I was blessed with a family.

In those early months after your birth, my world became wonderfully small. I was at home with you, not in vast landscapes, but in the slow, tiny world of a baby's. I had to learn to let go of needing to use every spare moment to research a new project, to be designing, to be studying, seeking, planning, running. To let go and just be, to let hours pass with nothing happening but watching my babies learn to roll, to smile, to start making sense of the world.

The way everyone told me that my life was going to completely change always felt like a dire warning. But I was a single mother running my own business. My life did change, but only for the better. I was no longer alone; there was suddenly purpose in everything I did.

When you were a few months old, I took you on our first trip with a cheerful nanny in tow. Now, we travel for my work, and I've watched you grow and become familiar with life in other cultures. I've also watched you learn to read, write, swim, climb, run; to find your sense of humour and your interests.

I have to travel alone at times. Then I struggle with the guilt of leaving you, knowing I am missing precious moments, and that you may be missing me at night. But this is who I am, how I survive and what I love.

Among all this joy is fear, an anxiety as I read the news, as friends discuss worrying political trends, as I witness the damage inflicted by climate change, as I see rows of young heads bowed over their phones.

I'm naturally nostalgic for the past, for slower, different ways of being and relating to the world. As an older mother, I can remember a computer-less, mobile-phone-less world and I'm not sure I like the new one we are creating. I have to believe there will be a turnaround, an awakening. That the world will pass through this dark moment and your generation will find a way to restore harmony, a place in which everyone and the natural world can co-exist.

With love, Muma xx

255

CLAIRE BRAYFORD

WRITER and BRAND CONSULTANT / Mother to CECILIA and URSULA

Claire Brayford was 22 when her career began, sorting swathes
of clothes in a windowless cupboard at a national newspaper.
She's now a fashion, beauty and lifestyle feature writer,
brand consultant and The Grace Tales' *UK editor.*
"I like the idea that style cannot be bought, but it can be learnt,"
says Claire. "I love to keep learning, discovering what's new and meeting
people who are passionate and truly knowledgeable in their
field. I find writing itself a bit like torture; however, as Dorothy Parker
put it, 'I hate writing, I love having written.'"

The mother of two girls, Claire's favourite quote on parenthood is from Bill Murray's
character, Bob Harris, in the film *Lost in Translation*: "Your life, as you know it...
is gone. Never to return. But they learn how to walk, and they learn how to talk...
and you want to be with them. And they turn out to be the most delightful
people you will ever meet in your life."

To my daughters, Cecilia and Ursula,

Through thick brown brambles at the end of the lane at my Granny's farmhouse in Ireland was an old, two-room stone cottage. From time to time, my cousins and I would cup our eyes to peer through the dirty window and glimpse an ordinary and everyday tableau frozen in time.

On the small wooden table by the window sat a bowl, a box of cornflakes and a spoon. A chair was pushed askew as if someone had risen quickly, and on the back hung a thick, wool jacket. For years, the scene remained undisturbed behind the heavy locked door.

We loved to speculate about who had lived there, why they had left and what else we would discover if we were able to step inside. We could have asked, but it was much more fun to imagine.

Until I was 16, I had only ever been to Ireland on holiday. I'd take an old pan from the kitchen and play 'house', peeling the potatoes in the barn. The hay barn was our shop and my sister and I would collect leaves and all the different apples that had fallen in the orchard to 'sell'.

We discovered an old oil lantern in one of the sheds and would go on adventures, freeing sheep from fences, if only we could find one.

My mum was one of seven children, and there were 12 cousins in total.

Sundays were Granny's favourite days. Everyone would get together and spend hours connecting the unwieldy Amstrad computer to her wood-clad television, only for it to be abandoned so we could go down to the end of the field and play on the rope swing.

She said the thing she looked forward to the most was for us all to be together. When she died, hundreds of people came to walk in silence behind her coffin.

I remember Granny's kindness, yet she never bought me anything. She kept a pair of scissors hidden in the airing cupboard so they would remain sharp, and only I was allowed to use them.

When I was at university, when 1940s-inspired bags were in style, she gave me one of her few black mock-croc frame designs from a wardrobe that smelt of mothballs.

Tuesdays, Thursdays and Saturdays were our favourite days, as the 'Bread Man' would arrive with his delivery of bread and pastries. He would wait patiently as the children deliberated the merits of each finger doughnut and its ratio of whipped cream to strawberry sauce.

In the evening, we would kneel down to say the Rosary and Granny would recite every saint by name. Then we would sit by the fire (and my brother would read his book).

They say it is the boring things you remember most. I wonder whether your childhood memories will be as mundane and as comforting as these are for me.

I pursued a career in fashion, a world away from my holidays in Ireland, but I hope that you will feel free enough to pursue, and take joy in, whatever it is that you decide to do and, with that, find happiness.

It's funny, because the word you probably hear the most – "careful" – is the last thing I want you to be.

Cecilia, you want to be an "explorer", and Ursula, you want to be a "man train driver", and I hope with all of my heart that you will be. That you will find your own kind of success and it will fill you with pride and contentment, and you will feel deserving of all the good things that will come your way.

Cecilia, you are gentle, thoughtful and imaginative. Ursula, you are spirited, determined and full of fun. You will share so much and you will complement, delight and exasperate each other in your difference.

I hope the memories we build now will make you resilient enough to survive the things I will not be able to protect you from.

And I hope that you have little girls whom you tell to be careful, but who you secretly hope are anything but.

Love, Mum

> *"I hope the MEMORIES we build now will make you RESILIENT enough to survive the things I will not be able to PROTECT you from."*

SALLY
OBERMEDER

MEDIA PERSONALITY, TELEVISION PRESENTER and CO-FOUNDER of lifestyle website SWIISH.COM / Mother to ANNABELLE and ELYSSA

"At first when I got the news, I was in utter shock. Then I just cried and cried. I was overcome with grief and it really took me a long time to accept it. Not only did I have to get my head around the fact that I had cancer at the age of 37, but I was also petrified I would be too sick to look after my newborn baby the way I wanted to." Sally Obermeder was diagnosed with breast cancer when she was 41 weeks' pregnant with her first child, Annabelle. She beat the disease and went on to have her second child, Elyssa, born via surrogate.

"While I had the best doctors, and friends and family rallied round and supported me... I ultimately discovered that there was no one who could fight the battle but me. I found a kind of strength and determination I have never felt before. But the flipside is that it taught me that life is delicate, precious and sacred. It's to be appreciated and enjoyed. It's a gift." Sally is uplifting, generous, funny and real. She's a hands-on mother, co-host of Channel 7's afternoon show *The Daily Edition*, and co-founder of fashion and lifestyle website SWIISH, which she runs with her best friend and sister Maha Koraiem. She has also published four books, *Never Stop Believing*, *Super Green Smoothies* (the bestselling smoothie book in Australia), *The Good Life* and, most recently, *Super Green: Simple and Lean*.

"The GREATEST thing that has ever happened TO ME was that you chose me to be YOUR MUM."

Dear Annabelle and Elyssa,

I feel so blessed you have each other – a best friend – for life. Your auntie Maha means the world to me. I think we probably speak to each other about 50 times a day! Your sister will always hold a mirror up to you. She will show you the best of you, but also show you where you're going wrong, and that's truly invaluable.

Annabelle, I often say to you: "You're so lucky. You don't even realise that you will have Elyssa for the rest of your life, a best friend who is going to understand everything about you, because she was there from the beginning." And you were – literally – you were at the birth of your baby sister. I say to your grandmother all the time, "The greatest gift you gave me was Maha."

Becoming a mother did not happen easily for me. Your dad and I tried so hard to become parents for seven years. Everyone around me was having babies at the drop of a hat without trying, and I felt like I was doing something wrong. I refused to do IVF, even though, in hindsight, I should have just done it years earlier. I finally wrapped my head around it and we did one cycle of IVF. And it worked. I was so fortunate.

One of the greatest experiences of my life was carrying you, Annabelle. I was deliriously happy. I had lots of energy, no morning sickness and worked right up until the end. I felt so full of life. I was at a place in my life where I felt like everything was coming together and everything was as it should be. I had a wonderful job, was in a very happy marriage and I was pregnant and soon to give birth. In that moment, so blissfully unaware of what was to come, I existed in a beautiful bubble.

At 41 weeks' pregnant I was diagnosed with stage 3 aggressive breast cancer. I endured eight months of intense chemotherapy, which started when you were 10 days old, Annabelle, and a double mastectomy. I didn't know how the story was going to end, if I was going to survive.

Annabelle, you were so little. You were just born, but you made me smile every day during my treatment and you gave me so much. I lived just for you. The power of a child is incredible. I was given the all-clear exactly one year from the day I received my life-changing diagnosis.

When I look back at that period of my life, my emotions are so mixed. Sometimes, I feel really teary and sad; sometimes, I have survivor guilt and feel that it's so unfair that there are so many amazing women out there who have lost their lives. Why did I survive?

Other times, I feel empowered by my strength and resilience. I feel so incredibly grateful that I'm still here,

I'm on the other side of it. Before cancer, I was tough on myself. I felt like I had to do more, achieve more. I've since silenced that inner critic and now I just do the best I can.

I'm generally a pretty happy person, which I think comes from having a happy childhood. But going through the cancer battle has made me more resilient and given me so much gratitude. I've experienced firsthand how you can wake up any day of the week and think it's a normal day, but, in fact, you have no control over what life has in store for you. I've experienced that there's no guarantee on tomorrow. You can think you know what you'll be doing six months from now, but there are no certainties. The only thing I know I have is, literally, the moment that I'm in.

I yearned for both of you so strongly and you both came into the world under unique circumstances. After you arrived, Annabelle, I knew I wanted to give you a sibling. After the cancer, I was told another natural pregnancy could cost me my life. I knew there would be a way and that, if I kept going, it would all work out. I just had that feeling.

Elyssa, our journey bringing you into the world wasn't easy. In fact, it was very complicated, from finding a surrogate to carry you in the United States, through the months that followed. When I speak to the extraordinary woman who carried you, Elyssa, I still cry. She is also a mother to four children and, for two years, she helped us grow our family. It was a big ask, but they gave us the gift of love, the gift of a child.

That type of kindness and generosity is something you can't even comprehend. How do you even repay someone like this? It's priceless. How amazing that there are people like her in this world, a woman from the other side of the globe whom I didn't even know, yet who would do this for our family.

I can barely remember who I was before I became a mother. The greatest thing that has ever happened to me was that you both chose me to be your mum. Every night, I'll walk around after I've put you both to bed and I just can't believe that I'm the mother of two children. It still takes my breath away after almost seven years.

Thank you – thank you for choosing me, and thank you for letting me love you and guide you through life. I don't think I really knew who I was until I became a mother. It is without a doubt my true life's purpose.

Love, Mum xxx

CATRIONA ROWNTREE

TV PRESENTER / Mother to ANDREW and CHARLIE

It's hard not to smile when talking to Catriona Rowntree. Her infectiously positive nature has the ability to turn anyone's frown upside down.
As a mother to two sons, the jet-setting TV presenter has mastered the fine art of mixing motherhood with work and travel, thanks to more than two decades at the helm of Australia's best loved travel show, Getaway.

"Where I go, they go (within reason), but I've no idea if they've inherited my wanderlust, as we're just out there doing it, travelling up a storm. I am so grateful for any opportunity to explore, to broaden my mind... and, above all, to never complain about where I live," she says. "Twenty-two years on, *Getaway* has confirmed to me that, even though Australia is not perfect, we have absolutely the most magnificent backyard that millions of people around the world would trade places for in a heartbeat."

While her family life on a Victorian farm is a far cry from the hustle and bustle of Sydney, the slower pace and focus on nature have had only a positive effect on the way she raises her sons. As with most mums juggling kids and career, she knows that routine and boundaries are the key to a happy and smoothly run home. "We have a small support team around us, but basically, my husband and I are a total team. Meals are eaten sitting down at the table; no TV on and definitely no devices at the table," she says.

Andrew and Charlie,

Sit down please, boys. Focus. I'd like to share some thoughts with both of you.

Andrew, you may remember I wrote you a letter just before your brother was born. I read it to you recently and you thought I was mad, but it was important to me that I wrote down my thoughts. I wanted you to know how much I love you, that I'll always be there for you, that you're a '24-hour Entertainment Machine' and that I can't imagine my heart stretching any more to love another child, as it's full to bursting with love for you. Do you remember this? Well, it turns out it could: my heart did stretch to include your very cheeky brother, Charlie, and I'm still sure it's going to burst, because I love you both so much.

Charlie, I need to include you now in this letter of love, so that we have documented evidence, a letter you can always go to whenever you feel like it, to be reminded that you will always have our support, protection and understanding. Do you understand this, boys? Good.

Just after I married your dad, things did feel different to me. Apart from the fact I'd left all my family in the city to move to a farm where I can't see any neighbours, where we have no asphalt to ride a bike on or any balconies to throw a ball off (these are your favourite things about my home in Sydney), I instantly felt Dad and I were a team.

It was exciting. It felt so good to have a person back me up, to support me, to laugh at my jokes, to do a silly dance around the kitchen with, to hold my hand when I needed an extra dollop of strength and, most of all, to give me big cuddles. Well guess what? You're now on that team with us, too. We are a total team of four and, together, we are unbeatable.

Why? Because each of us knows we will always be there for each other, loved for who we are and 110 per cent supported in all that we choose to do. Go, team!

Are you still listening, boys? Good. Dad and I feel very fortunate that every day we are able to show you how we can make our passions our professions. We think it's our job to find that little quirk in you, to find what makes your heart sing and bring that to the fore. Being a palaeontologist, being a professional soccer player – you go for it, baby!

Dad wants you to know that sometimes it may feel like we are picking on you: like when we ask you to stop eating with your mouth open or picking your nose. Or when we say, "Close the door! Were you born in a tent?" I will not delete this from the letter, boys, because we want the best for you.

When I was growing up, the same thing happened to me. But I was so lucky The Stork dropped me off into that family. To have a Nan who made me feel that I was loved unconditionally, who taught me the importance of always choosing kindness and learning to love the dictionary! To have a mum who always made sure we had good manners, were respectful of others and bought me the best shoes. To have a dad whom I could call on and talk to no matter what time of the day, and who taught me the importance of writing thank-you letters. Boy, was I lucky to feel their love. Even if I was on the other side of the world, doing my job "going off talking", I knew I had my family of cheerleaders. And that's exactly what you have in us. Yes, we are your cheerleaders!

We may not always *literally* (your current favourite word) be right by your side, but in your mind, in your heart, you know we are there. As Dad says, "Here come the kisses."

Those kisses will never stop. Charlie, when you're having "the worst day ever!", here come the kisses. Andrew, if someone else upsets you, here come the kisses. You will have blue days, my darlings, not feeling very good about yourself, and you will have days when you feel amazing, "like John Cena!", yes! And always, we will be there for you, saying, "Here come the kisses."

We love every spare centimetre of you both... Here come the kisses.

Love, Mum

ACKNOWLEDGEMENTS

This book is a wonderful collaboration between almost 100 women – photographers, writers, editors, art directors, hair stylists, makeup artists and more – from around the world. It is a tome to treasure and a testament to what can be achieved when women come together. Magic happens – and when most of those women are mothers, it happens quickly...

We are so grateful to our fantastic publisher, Sally Eagle, who recognised our vision from the beginning and gave us the chance to bring it to life. To our art director, Hannah Blackmore, whose exquisite style and taste shines through every page. What a pleasure it was to work with someone who 'got' our vision from day dot. To our editor, Sally Feldman, for pulling it all together with such poise, precision and elegance. We couldn't have done this without these three incredible women.

To the wonderful photographers who have contributed to this book – Hellene Algie, Corrie Bond, Brigitte Lacombe, Alice Whitby, Helene Sandberg, Anna Huix, Sarah Wood, David Loftus, Erika Lane, Daniel Nadel, Liz Ham, Bridget Wood, Zeynel Abidin, Yumi Matsuo, Rachel Jackson and Lauren Webb – it is an honour to have your beautiful images in *Grace Mothers*. Thank you.

To all the women who have shared their heartfelt letters and opened their hearts to us; who let us into their homes. We connect through sharing our vulnerabilities – so thank you for being honest. Each letter is an absolute joy to read and a reminder that we each have our own unique journey.

To the team behind *The Grace Tales* – our editor-at-large, Emily Armstrong, the visionary who makes things happen – talented, smart, energetic and the driving force behind so much of what we do. Jenny Guo, for keeping the wheels turning – what a spectacularly talented individual you are. Marisa Remond, for your fantastic style and engaging stories. And Amy Malpass Hahn, for your immense passion and incredible talent. Thank you for everything you all do for the brand.

To the creatives who work with Julie Adams Photography – Hellene Algie, René Norwie and Paula Maloney. Thank you for all your support in bringing this project to life and for your immense passion for your craft.

To Rob McCourt, for everything you do, always, and Chris McCourt, for being an incredible mentor.

To our dear families, because, as much as we love our work, nothing matters more in life than our relationships. We love you all dearly.

Most of all, to our darling children – there are six between the three authors, all, funnily enough, spirited little girls – Arabella, Lottie, Maddie, Vivi, Cecilia and Ursula. We love you to the moon and back. This book is for all of you. Go for it girls – you can achieve anything you put your minds to.

Published in 2019 by Bauer Media Books, Australia Bauer Media Books is a division of Bauer Media Pty Ltd

THE GRACE TALES

Founder Georgie Abay
Photographer Julie Adams
Editor-in-chief Amy Malpass Hahn
Editor-at-large Emily Armstrong
Editorial director Marisa Remond
Business executive Jenny Guo
UK editor Claire Brayford

BAUER MEDIA BOOKS

Publisher Sally Eagle
Creative director Hannah Blackmore
Editor Sally Feldman

Photography Julie Adams
Additional photography
Corrie Bond (p 4), Hellene Algie (pp 10-11), Brigitte Lacombe (pp 48-49), Alice Whitby (pp 56-59, 228-231), Helene Sandberg (pp 68-71, 102-105, 114-119, 124, 140-143, 216-217, 256), Anna Huix (p84), Sarah Wood (pp 86-91), David Loftus (p 106), Erika Lane (pp 170-173), Daniel Nadel (p 178), Liz Ham (pp 180-185), Bridget Wood (pp 202-205, 248-251), Zeynel Abidin (p 210), Yumi Matsuo (pp 238-241), Rachel Jackson (p 242), Lauren Webb (pp 252-255)

Published by Bauer Media Books,
a division of Bauer Media Pty Ltd,
54 Park St, Sydney; GPO Box 4088,
Sydney, NSW 2001, Australia
phone +61 2 9282 8618; fax +61 2 9126 3702
www. thegracetales.com.au

Bauer Media Pty Limited 2019
ABN 18 053 273 546

Printed in China by 1010 Printing International

A catalogue record for this book is available
from the National Library of Australia.
ISBN: 978-1-92569-466-6